The Secret of Anzio Bay

*A flyer's Italian wartime adventures
are revealed by the plane
he crash-landed fifty-four years earlier*

by Michael Mauritz

with Francine Bartolacci Costello

The Secret of Anzio Bay

Cover design by Kathy Pater, Word Association Publishers
Cover photo by Paolo Varriale

Word Association Publishers
205 Fifth Avenue
Tarentum, Pennsylvania 15084
800-827-7903
www.wordassociation.com

Lieutenant Michael Mauritz, 1943

We speak of "Skipper" as if it had a soul. To reunite it with the man who piloted it on that fatal day is a great opportunity to bear witness to the historical value of the events which have marked the century. The arrival of Lt. Michael Mauritz from the past is a great step in the history of Piana delle Orme Museum.

Alda Dalzini, Piana delle Orme Museum, 1998

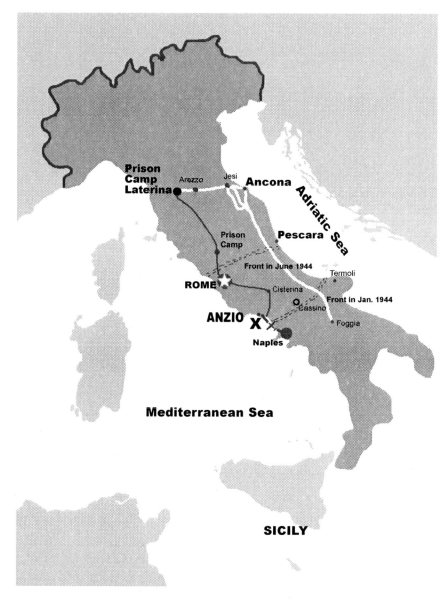

Italy, January, 1944

X marks the spot where *Skipper* was put down. The black line represents the distance we were trucked as prisoners; Anzio to Rome, Rome to the first prison camp and finally to the camp at Laterina. The white line indicates the route we took on foot after our escape.

To all the kind and generous Italian people
who fed me, housed me, nursed me through illness,
and risked their lives for five months
to help me return home.
And heartfelt gratitude to
Mariano de Pasquale
and his beautiful
Piana delle Orme Museum—*Skipper*'s home

Salute!

With great appreciation we acknowledge
the splendid work of Word Association's dedicated and
talented editor, Nan Newell. Her expertise, diligence and
patience is unequaled.

Some of the names of people and places have
been changed to protect the privacy of those who
did not have the opportunity to give
permission for their inclusion in this book.

FOREWORD

After September 11, 2001

Listening to National Public Radio one morning near the end of October, I heard about a group of artists who had been given studio space near the top of one of the towers of the World Trade Center. The thinking was that the magnificent views and perspectives would inspire these artists in new ways. And in typically American fashion the inspiration was not only transcendent but brilliantly diverse. One musician attached microphones to the windows and captured the sound of the wind buffeting the tower along with a few stray and distorted human noises that had drifted upward. Another artist had planned to reflect the sterility of corporate America through her work. But long before September 11th, she found herself abandoning her project as she came to know a few of the inhabitants of the tower. Some, she said, played tag in the halls. Others never failed to nod good morning. The World Trade Center, she came to learn, was in every sense a community of middle-class people, going about their daily lives, being neighborly, making friends, making a living.

On that bright blue morning when the towers were viciously destroyed, only two artists were in the studio. One of them had recently completed a painting of a World War II era Tuskegee Airman as the martyred Saint Sebastian. But instead of the pilot being pierced by arrows, the airman was pierced by tiny airplanes.

Although the hijacked plane crashed very near the studio, one of the artists somehow made her way down through the devastation to safety. The artist who was moved to paint his version of Saint Sebastian was not so fortunate.

Like everyone else, I have many emotions and thoughts about the brutal attack on our beloved country. When I was able to relate it to my own war experience and the incredible set of circumstances that led me to write this book, I thought again of the artist who had been killed there. I wondered how the idea had come to him to create such a prophetic painting. And I think I know.

After eighty years of living, I don't believe in coincidences. I believe in destiny. I believe that evil exists in this world as an entity that is separate and apart from God. Evil is the very absence of God. We have the power to avoid it, fight it, learn from it, and even grow and flower in spite of it. All of that, I believe, comes from God—a God who perhaps whispers a warning in the form of a vision, a God who positions courageous people to rush to the rescue of others with no thought of their own safety, a God, who perhaps prepares someone to leave this earth by leading him to create a painting with a prophetic message.

This story of mine is small and personal. It is from a past war that now seems more comprehensible than this new war. But in these days when we have seen heroes come forward when heroes are most needed, I am grateful that the story I have to tell is one of courage, compassion, and generosity at a time when darkness nearly succeeded. From the beginning I felt sure that I was led to tell this story, and now in these troubled times, I know it is even more important that I do so, because goodness and human solidarity are always what count most.

God Bless America
Michael Mauritz

Introduction

Most of us carry certain places in our minds and our hearts—places where we rounded a bend and stepped into a time when life got turned up a notch. The images are still sharp, fine-tuned by that part of our brain that records our lives and makes an imprint on our souls as indelible as a tattoo. What was part of us then remains a part of us now. Even if we don't think about that time consciously or even if we resist remembering, it is always there, in place and intact, whether we like it or not.

Some of us live like this with particular memories which, I suspect, can haunt us, dog us, or delight us into eternity. Almost at will or sometimes against our will, again and again, we walk those remembered rooms or streets, see the faces, hear the sounds, recall the scents, the voices—whatever and whomever it was that set the stage and assembled the cast for each memory that we carry. So much stays with us that it may be hard to believe that some part of us is not still there.

The author Isak Dinesen, who wrote *Out of Africa*, a memoir about her beloved farm in Kenya, wondered—decades after leaving the farm—if that place, which had meant so much to her and had lived so fully in her memory, had any memory of her. It was obvious that she wasn't referring to the physical evidence of her presence there, like her house or her gardens; rather, she was hinting at something more mystical, something subtle within us and our experience that is whispered back across the long, rugged terrain of time. It's like the feeling you get when you go back to visit your childhood home where strangers are now living. You look for some indefinable thing that connects you to that place. It isn't the built-in bookcase that your father made or the wallpaper in the dining room; no, it's something much more. Dinesen considered that it might be the memory of her shadow walking along her drive.

But things and places don't remember us. We are left to remember them. At least that's what I thought.

———

Footprints are something no fighter pilot ever intends to leave behind. His job is to stay high above the battlefield, then swoop down on his target and vanish without a trace. If a fighter pilot leaves his footprints on a wartorn earth, he is most likely walking with death hot on his heels. But in wartime a soldier doesn't control his destiny. Finally what happens, happens. And then, if he survives, it's over and he goes on with his life and he thinks that that part of his journey is complete.

He thinks.

An All-American Fighter

Skipper. How jaunty. A plane named *Skipper.* A fighter plane.

Skipper. It has a Knute Rockney "can do" kind of sound. It smacks of a "down home in Indiana" attitude. Makes you want to have a cuppa Joe, wear a hat cocked to one side, and smoke a Lucky Strike out of the corner of your mouth. It puts you in a Glenn Miller state of mind.... "The touch of your hand on a June night, that moonlight serenade..." Perfect lyrics and perfect harmony, smooth as a malted shake.

Skipper. It's every World War II movie you ever saw. It swaggers and swings with an exclusively American, boyish bravado. Like young Frank Sinatra himself. Three parts ruffian, one part choirboy. Gary Cooper and his kind, putting "Jerry" in his place.

Skipper. It paints a Norman Rockwell picture of those flyers, those young, very young, smooth-faced American survivors of the Depression, those young men who knew what it was to be a little bit hungry and sometimes a lot poor. Some of them came through childhoods wearing hand-me-downs, "doing without." They were the "fly boys," the daring young men in their flying machines. They could taunt death up there, because they didn't believe they could die when they were fighting for "Right"—just like those Saturday-matinee cowboys they had idolized.

Skipper. It's an all-American, sweet-sounding, white-bread name, a name that, along with all the others like it, has its place in the annals of this war. Like the young Americans who

1

crossed oceans to fight and sometimes die. "Crazy" was what Joseph Heller called them in his '60s novel, *Catch-22*. Heller wrote that World War II flyers were not permitted to fly unless they were judged mentally healthy. But he concluded that, to fly in that war in those dangerous missions, a pilot would have to be crazy or he couldn't have done it. And that, according to Heller, was "Catch-22." You cannot fly if you're crazy, but you would not fly if you were not crazy! Maybe Heller's "crazy" was just courage, confidence or, as the song goes, "cockeyed optimism." Crazy or not, these young, brash Americans made their mark in the great struggles and left an enduring impression. A wholly American impression of youth, courage, humor, and honor that would endure long after the "boys"—those who survived—were back on their own soil and had become old men.

How could the cocky young Yank who had the name *Skipper* painted on the side of his Curtiss P-40 Warhawk ever dream that its destiny would be to lie dormant in Italian waters for over half a century? Staying behind long after the last American soldier had gone home a victor, leaving the Italians and much of the world a legacy of swing, chewing gum, and not a few fatherless babies. The war in Europe ended. Headlines announced the bombing of Hiroshima. Peace was declared. But the sea would continue to hold *Skipper* captive. There it lay, silent and waiting, under Anzio Bay, while Korea ignited a new kind of world conflict and Americans were transfixed by television. As a cold war divided Berlin and the planet, the fighter sank deeper into the wet sand. The Red Scare was everywhere. The great powers raced for the moon and aimed nuclear weapons at each other. But under the bay *Skipper* remained in darkness, not far from the famous golden Italian beaches, which were once again drawing pale tourists from everywhere. While Italy was exporting its food, fashion and movie stars, seaweed and kelp covered the old fighter plane in the bay. The great Italian ship *Andrea Doria* sank. A boy named Elvis emerged as the king of "Rock 'n' Roll." Then as sand seeped deeper into *Skipper*'s belly, a young American president was assassinated. Americans fell in love with Gina, Sophia, and Marcello. Four young men from England revolutionized popular music, a civil war in southeast Asia nearly tore our nation in two—and still, Anzio Bay kept its little secret. We learned about marriage and "Divorce Italian Style." As salt water faded *Skipper*'s desert camouflage, black Americans rose up and demanded equal rights. Computers ran the world. Italians forgot their dialects. And while western civilization prepared for a new millennium, Mediterranean currents at last conspired with the shifting sands as Nature herself decreed that *Skipper*'s time had come.

Return from the Sea

1998

Italians, fishing illegally in an area restricted for use by the Italian Air Force, complained, unofficially, that their nets were getting caught on something in the bay just south of Anzio.

It was known by some, and maybe even by many, that an American plane had gone down in these waters during the war. No big surprise. Italy has many such mementos but this particular plane would have a mission well beyond the war.

An organization called Archeosub, a group of retired Italian military officers who are divers by avocation, had gone down to look at the plane. Not a very taxing dive, for the plane rested in only thirty feet of water. But what they saw excited them. Unlike many war artifacts under the Italian sea, this plane was intact. It appeared that it had not crashed into the bay but had somehow and for some reason made a deliberate landing, and had done so gracefully and with great skill.

Now they had to find someone with the resources to bring the plane up. Here Fate begins to spin her magic, drawing together the perfect fit of people, places, and events. Enter Mariano de Pasquale, a figure well known in the Anzio region as a self-made multimillionaire with an expensive hobby.

When De Pasquale was a child in wartime Sicily, General Patton and his troops passed his doorstep. Awestruck, young Mariano watched as GIs set up their big guns and spent the day blasting the Germans from his island home. He never forgot the American soldiers who came to his door at the end

4

of that day.

Here was this skinny little boy with dark curls and wide almond eyes, standing on a chair beside his mother as she cautiously opened a window only slightly to see who was banging at her door. This is a boy with almost no memory of life without war. Soldiers, tanks, thundering explosions are his life.

"*Chi bussa alla porta?*" asks Mariano's mother.

"*Scusi*, ma'am, I mean *signora*, please, food? Mun-ja? Hungry, I mean, *molto fame*! Ah...food, we need food. I—I mean, we—can pay for it. *Soldi*, I think that's the word. *Soldi* for the food." The soldier, holding money in his hand, extends it toward the woman. "You understand? *Fame*—we can pay for the food. *Soldi*—pay for the food with *soldi*, understand?"

The young man speaking to the boy's mother is a tall American soldier with big white teeth and blue eyes. His face is dirty, but he is smiling and gesturing with his hands, rubbing his stomach, pretending to be eating.

"*Si*," she says cautiously, "*fame. Si.*" Speaking slowly in Italian in hopes that the young soldier might understand her, she repeats, "You're hungry and want me to give you food, yes? And you are saying that you want to *pay* for the food?"

The soldier, recognizing some of the words, nods vigorously.

"Mother of God, he is *asking* for food and offering money!" Turning to Mariano, she whispers, "These American soldiers are nothing like those Germans who just helped themselves to our food!"

The next day the Americans were gone. In fact, it seemed the war was gone. No noise. No shelling, no trucks, no soldiers. So the little boy was allowed to venture outside of his house and into the quiet. He could walk over to the places where the soldiers had been and think about all he had seen and heard. He could pretend he was one of them, a *soldato americano*, lounging against a tree, stretching out his long legs while eating his mother's goat cheese and bread. They had laughed as they tossed a tightly wadded undershirt back and forth as if it were a ball. "Bas-i-bal," he remembered them calling their game. As he wandered, he found a box and some spent shells left behind by the *soldati,* the tall, smiling American soldiers who had been so respectful to his mother. Maybe the blue-eyed soldier who had come to the door left this box and the shells for Mariano as a present! So he took them for himself, these mementos of the *americani.* And in that moment he spawned an obsession and a collection that fifty years into the future would be worth nearly thirty million dollars.

After the war, the De Pasquales left Sicily for northern Italy, where they farmed. Later, the grown Mariano de Pasquale purchased land in Latina not far from Anzio and began growing flowers. Because he was hard-working, smart and aggressive, De Pasquale's flower farm prospered and grew. And while he was becoming one of Europe's largest flower producers, De Pasquale continued to amass what would become one of the world's largest private collections of World War II military artifacts. When producers were making the Academy-Award-winning films *Life Is Beautiful* and *The English Patient*, it was De Pasquale who was able to rent them the vintage World War II jeeps they needed for their movies. When filmmakers explained that one of De Pasquale's precious jeeps would have to be blown up for a scene in *The English Patient*, De Pasquale was unfazed; he merely collected all of the fragments of the jeep and created for his new museum a scene depicting a jeep destroyed by the enemy.

But it was the museum, Piana delle Orme ("The Plain of Footsteps"), that convinced the Archeosub divers that Mariano de Pasquale might be the one to finance the second dive to salvage the well-preserved plane in Anzio Bay. What an addition this fighter plane would make to the famous De Pasquale collection that was now housed in his museum. And so De Pasquale agreed, and the dive had its backer. If all went well, Mariano de Pasquale would have a centerpiece for his beautiful sixteen-building Piana delle Orme Museum that sits like a jewel among his fields of flowers in Latina.

———

Early on the morning of January 10, 1998, divers began the arduous struggle to bring the aircraft (twice its normal weight) to the surface. Even without the three tons of sand filling its belly, the Curtiss P-40L was a heavy craft. It was dubbed "Gypsy Rose Lee" during the war when U. S. military-aircraft manufacturers tried to lighten the slow-moving plane by "stripping" it of all nonessentials. Despite their efforts, the Curtiss P-40L was still heavy and slow, no real match for the feisty British Spitfires or dreaded German Messerschmidts. But what the P-40 lacked in speed it had in endurance. Carrying six fifty-caliber Browning machine guns and often a bomb, the Curtiss could take a lot of hits. And this one did. There were bullet holes in its belly and a piece missing from its tail. Then, of course, there was this landing in Anzio Bay and fifty-four years under the sea. Some tough craft!

As the day wore on, divers became more and more frustrated in their efforts to bring the plane to the surface. Finally, as the light was beginning to fade, they achieved success. They had been trying to raise the craft by attaching huge yellow balloons to it. Usually two are enough to bring up the types of

7

wreckage they were used to retrieving. But by now they had attached fourteen balloons to the plane, each strapped one to another, and at last it began to float to the surface. As they reached shallower water, they placed a skid under the craft and pulled it ashore. At first, the plane, with its tail still submerged, looked broken and helpless. Surrounded by divers, belly on wet sand, it lay there barnacled and encrusted by decades under the Mediterranean.

In photographs and on the video, you see in the distance a large crowd coming to witness the retrieval of this World War II relic. The Italian news media had picked up the story of a well-preserved American plane being resurrected from Anzio Bay by a millionaire farmer for his museum in Latina. The pictures show people climbing over the dunes. They are coming across a beach that appears unchanged from the long war years when Anzio earned its place in modern history as the scene of one of the fiercest battles of World War II.

Finally the plane is completely out of the water. Now it appears to have regained some of its former strength and spirit. It is, after all, a creature of the air, and rescue from the water has already transformed it. The craft is immediately proclaimed in remarkable condition, indicating that it had been landed in the bay and not crashed! The crowd, an estimated five thousand, maintains a respectful distance, as if the remains of the pilot might still be in the cockpit. But this plane is all there is. The pilot is long gone, his fate a mystery. The plane has to tell its story alone for now and, like a suspect offered immunity, it sings like a bird.

A parachute is pulled from an air-intake scoop designed to cool the engine.

From the beginning, Italian officials saw the spectacle

of the plane's recovery as a potential disaster. First, the beach and dunes in this region are an ecologically fragile and necessarily protected area. This beach area, being part of a military installation used by the Italian Air Force, is off limits to civilians. And then there was the plane itself. Because it was a war plane, live ammunition could still have been aboard. Nevertheless, the people came in droves to see. These Italians, many or most of whom weren't even born before the end of the war, wanted to see. In the photographs they appear to have the same look as those who have caught a glimpse of something new, different, or foreign that has made a sudden, surprise appearance, like a UFO that drops from the sky or a whale that washes up on the beach. Like the munchkins in *The Wizard of Oz* venturing out to see Dorothy's house when it fell on the Wicked Witch. It may be the strangeness of the thing itself, but more likely it is the incongruity of the thing in relation to place or time.

And yet this plane is deeply connected to the Italians. Even though generations separate them, there is an abiding relationship. This is an American plane, a symbol of the American presence and the great Allied military force that pushed the Germans from Italy, ending its long, dark nightmare. It was the Americans, many Italians believe, who brought order, justice, sustenance, and liberty to a beleaguered Italy half a century ago.

———

It was nearly dark and the plane would have to be left on the beach, guarded, until the next day when it would be trucked to the Piana delle Orme Museum (about twenty miles as the crow flies). But the story has already begun to come into focus. The mysterious wreckage in Anzio Bay is not such a mystery anymore. It is an American-made Curtiss P-40L Warhawk, with the name *Skipper* on its side. Several bullet holes are found on the side of the plane near its markings. It is carrying six loaded machine guns. There is no bomb aboard. The cockpit bears the name and serial number of its regularly assigned flyer, Lieutenant E. E. Parsons. But even while *Skipper* is being transported to its home at Piana delle Orme, a researcher has already discovered that this plane was not landed in Anzio Bay by any E. E. Parsons.

The next day Mariano de Pasquale supervised as his museum workers carefully lowered *Skipper* into a pool of fresh water in an attempt to remove the salt. There the craft would remain until the workers discovered that the fresh water was actually causing further damage. And so *Skipper* was allowed to dry out and retain its sea-encrusted look.

Timing, coincidence, and fate seem to be in league to bring this story to life.

———

Now enter Ferdinando d'Amico, amateur historian, author, and specialist on the air war in Italy. He makes his home in a small village near Florence and works for the Italian government's Labor Inspectorate. D'Amico is another whose passion is his avocation. Like Mariano de Pasquale, his love of military history began in childhood. Unlike Mariano de Pasquale, D'Amico was born long after the war ended—not until 1955. His love of aviation history started with the building of plastic model-airplane kits. As his interest grew, he began to research the subject in order to build better, more authentic models. In time D'Amico's research became so sophisticated that he began to piece together details on the air war that had never before been published. Soon he and a fellow military-aviation history enthusiast began publishing books on the subject. To date, D'Amico has four books to his credit and many more articles in magazines devoted to military history. It is no wonder that the divers of Archeosub who first went down to look at the wreckage in Anzio Bay sought out D'Amico to do the research on the plane.

It was Archeosub's Piero Faggioli who first contacted D'Amico just after New Year's. Faggioli phoned to tell him about a dive in Anzio Bay that had located an American fighter plane. He briefed him on the plans to recover the plane on January 10. Faggioli wanted to know if D'Amico would help them identify the craft. He was able to tell the historian that the plane was a Curtiss P-40. He gave him the serial number of the fighter and told him that the name Parsons was painted beneath the cockpit with *Skipper* painted on the right side of the cowling.

D'Amico possesses an extensive collection of military documents as well as dozens of microfilm rolls purchased from the United States Air Force Historical Research Center. Most of these documents consist of operational diaries of U. S. Air Force units in Italy during World War II.

You might think that a search for *Skipper*'s history would involve D'Amico sifting through miles of microfilm to locate this particular fighter plane among the hundreds and hundreds in service in Italy during the war. Not in this story. According to D'Amico, the very first roll he checked contained, incredibly, the list of missing air crew. Just like that! This list identified all of the planes lost by the U. S. Air Force in World War II. Now D'Amico was able to determine that the P-40 in the bay belonged to the 79th Fighter Group, 86th Fighter Squadron, and that it was lost on January 31, 1944.

Next he examined a roll containing the diaries of the 79th. At first the unit's list of losses didn't show any planes missing on January 31, 1944. A dead end. But several days later, D'Amico went back into his microfilm rolls and almost by accident noticed, at the end of one roll, a document reporting that on "31 January 1944" a plane flown by Lieutenant Michael Mauritz had been forced to ditch off Anzio due to engine trouble. "So," he said, "now I have the name of the pilot, and it wasn't Parsons!"

All of this was accomplished by our skilled historian while *Skipper* was still resting in the sea near the Anzio beach.

Armed with the name Michael Mauritz, D'Amico found a Web site listing the names of everyone in the United States in the white pages. Quickly he scrolled to the M's. M-a, M-a-u, M-a-u-r-i-t-z! Mauritz, Michael! There were just five of them in the United States! But fifty-four years have gone by. If the Michael Mauritz who landed a plane in Anzio Bay even survived the war, was he alive now? How old would he be today? Was he living in the United States? Did he even have a telephone listing? Suppose none of the five Michael Mauritzes was the one he was looking for—there was only one way to find out. So to the first Michael Mauritz in Turtle Creek, Pennsylvania, the second in West Jordan, Utah, the third in Lakewood, Colorado, the fourth in Neenah, Wisconsin, and the fifth in Platteville, Wisconsin, Ferdinando d'Amico composed, in his very proper, if not somewhat stilted and sometimes faltering, English, this heartfelt letter:

Carmignano, 20 January 1998

Dear Mr. Mauritz,

First of all, let me ask you to forgive me if I'm disturbing you without even knowing if you are the person I'm trying to contact! After this strange beginning, let me introduce myself: I am an Italian aviation historian and from over twenty years I have been working on the study of the aerial operations that took place in Italy from 1943 to 1945.

I've also published several books both in the U. S. and in England about this very subject. What brought me to write this letter to you, however, was caused by an event that took place a few weeks ago and which I was involved into: the rescue of a Curtiss P-40 fighter from the sea near Anzio.

A few weeks ago I was contacted by a search divers team to identify the submerged plane on the basis of the data found on the fuselage (no pictures were then available, so I hadn't yet seen personally the plane). This is what I discovered by searching through both the 79th FG and the 86th FS diaries.

The P-40L Serial Number 42-10857 belonged to 79th FG, 86th FS, Coded X4, and bore the nickname *Skipper* on port side. It was the personal mount of Lieutenant E. E. Parsons (his name being painted ahead of the cockpit). On January 31, 1944, however, it wasn't flown by him. On board there was instead 2/Lt. Michael Mauritz who, during an armed reconnaissance mission over Anzio beachhead, was apparently hit by some groundfire. The engine seized and the pilot was compelled to effect a perfect ditching very near the shore line. Last time he was seen he had reached the shore and was trying to hide in a bush with German troops heading towards him. He was listed as Missing in Action (presumably Prisoner of War).

The plane has been successfully recovered and brought on the shore virtually intact and in really remarkable conditions; a filmed reportage on the recovery of the P-40 has been aired on Italian TV Sunday evening.

I don't know if the real Michael Mauritz is still alive and if he survived to the capture and the imprisonment. What I do know, however, is that I had to try to locate him or some of his relatives in the U. S. The first step was to search the U. S. "white pages" to look for all those named "Michael Mauritz" and I've been lucky, since in all the U.S. there are only five of them!

So here I am writing to you this letter, in the hope that you could be "that" Michael Mauritz who, fifty four years ago, ditched his P-40 near Anzio and whose airplane is today once again "alive and kicking." It would be nonetheless great if you are one of his relatives and could help me to locate him and/or his family.

It would be extremely pleasing for me and for all those who worked to rescue the P-40, if the original pilot of the plane or someone of his family could eventually attend to the ceremony that will be made once the restoration will be completed and, considering the amazingly good state of the aircraft, this will not take many years.

I hope that you could help me to bring back together the man and the machine and, while thanking you for your kind attention and patience in reading me so far, I wait for your welcome reply and remain with

> Kindest regards,
> Ferdinando d'Amico

Anzio to Oklahoma and Back

In the days following the January 10, 1998, recovery of *Skipper*, Italian Air Force Colonel Euro Rossi and two of his lieutenants who had participated in the dive were doing some internet surfing of their own, searching out information on the P-40. Their search led them to one Boyd Fallwell of Oklahoma, a self-styled patriot, and his Veterans Honor Guard Web site.

Boyd Fallwell, now sixty-six years old, was drafted into the army in the 1950s and served as a military policeman in Texas during the Korean War. In his rich drawl the Oklahoman says flat out, "I served gladly, but I did not like the military. I threw my uniforms away and everything." Boyd went on to become a mechanic, living his civilian life without ever giving a thought to the military he was so glad to leave. A massive heart attack in 1990 would launch Fallwell into the destiny for which he was apparently born. He would survive his heart attack, but would now have a deadly condition called ventricular tachycardia that led him into several near-death episodes and had him in and out of Veterans Hospital for nearly a year. Lying in the hospital, Fallwell said he had plenty of time to think. He was surrounded by veterans of all ages, suffering and dying from all manner of illness and injury. "I learned to love those guys," he said. In the process he came to know and love the Lord.

Once back at home and no longer able to work, Fallwell joined a disabled veterans group who provided military honor-guard services at the funerals of veterans. In five years Fallwell served at some 250 funerals and became honor guard captain. Then in 1995 a combination of disagreements and the failing health of aging veterans who could no longer attend the funerals convinced Fallwell to break from the veterans group and go off on his own as a one-man honor guard at the funerals. Since 1995 Fallwell has gone on to do another 320 funerals on his own. "It's become my ministry," he said. In fact the Reverend Dave Mosier of Arlington National Cemetery has officially made Fallwell a lay minister. "Now," Fallwell said, "when the preacher don't show up, it gives me a chance to get in a few words about Jesus."

So focused was he on what he calls his honor-guard ministry that in 1995 he put a page on the World Wide Web to memorialize veterans. To date, his eighty-page-plus site has had over thirty-seven thousand visitors who travel through cyberspace to pay honor to Fallwell's departed veterans.

Among those thousands were Colonel Rossi and his lieutenants, who were looking for an American pilot named E. E. Parsons who had crash-landed his Curtiss P-40L into Anzio Bay.

It was just the kind of thing Boyd Fallwell loves to do. Fallwell had long ago come to rely upon the wealth of information available through Lynn Gamma and the United States Air Force Historical Agency.

Her response, thanks to the declassification of war documents, was just what Ferdinando D'Amico had learned weeks earlier: E. E. Parsons, now deceased, had not been at the stick on the last day *Skipper* was flown. The Curtiss P-40, she said, was taken on its last mission on January 31, 1944, by a Lieutenant Michael Mauritz. Just as quick as that, Fallwell was given a full account of Lieutenant Mauritz and how he came to crash-land *Skipper* in the bay.

The report went on to say that Michael Mauritz had been serving with the U. S. Air Corps 79th Fighter Group, 86th

Fighter Squadron, at Capodichino Landing Ground near Naples. According to records, he departed Capodichino on a course of 290 degrees bound for the Anzio-Nettuno area on a fighter patrol in formation. Weather conditions and visibility on that day were 10/10 at 1500 with poor visibility. The report confirmed that Mauritz was piloting the same P-40L that had been recovered from the bay. Fallwell further learned that the craft had six caliber-50 Browning machine guns and one person on board. And that person, the pilot, a Lieutenant Michael Mauritz, Serial Number 0-687390, was officially listed as a battle casualty.

According to records, the formation had been flying at an altitude of eight hundred feet with a target of the Anzio beachhead. Mauritz's aircraft reportedly left formation south of Anzio, one mile south of the fighting front. A witness, Air Corps Major Melvin Nielsen, who was the squadron leader, reported that Lieutenant Mauritz made an emergency landing in the water near the beach at G-068110 after radioing that his coolant temperature had reached 150 degrees centigrade. Nielsen, who left formation to look after the unfortunate pilot, said he witnessed Mauritz make a successful dead-stick belly landing in shallow water near the beach after dropping his fuel tank in the water. Major Nielsen wrote that he watched as Mauritz got out of his nearly submerged airplane and waded ashore. Nielsen said he saw Mauritz reach the beach and hide himself in some low bushes.

But then Nielsen described a disturbing scene. "I saw a man wearing a helmet. He was moving cautiously through the bushes near where Lieutenant Mauritz was hidden." Nielsen noted that at this point his fuel was getting low, forcing him to leave the area and proceed with the mission. He saw no more of Mauritz.

In response to Mauritz's initial radio report, a rescue launch arrived at the beach shortly after Nielsen left, in hopes of retrieving the young lieutenant.

Now the military reports shift from Nielsen's account to Air Corps Operations Officer Captain George W. Ewing, Jr., of the 79th Fighter Group. It appears that Captain Ewing and a Flight Officer Wall flew over the scene shortly after eleven that morning and observed the launch as it approached the beach. According to Captain Ewing, two men from the launch conducted an extensive search of the area, yelling and whistling for Mauritz. They walked inland, Ewing said, beyond the road nearest the shore where Mauritz had been seen on the beach by Major Nielsen. But with no success. When the rescue personnel reboarded their launch, Wall established radio contact with them and learned that they had found a "Mae West" (a life jacket) and an uninflated dinghy. They reported that the Mae West had no blood on it. They also said they had requested permission to search four houses on the road northwest of the spot where Lieutenant Mauritz had gone down. But by that time the launch was being fired upon and so they dropped the request. Flight Officer Wall strafed the houses and left the scene, concluding the search for Lieutenant Mauritz.

Lieutenant Michael Mauritz would officially be listed as "missing in action." His family would be notified. His personal belongings would be packed and sent home to Pennsylvania. Among them would be a journal Michael had been keeping.

So it was Fallwell's turn to log on to switchboard.com. Moments later the Oklahoma patriot learned about the five Michael Mauritzes in the United States. Much too impetuous to write letters, Fallwell picked up the phone and called the first one on the list.

A Bolt from Heaven

1921, Turtle Creek, Pennsylvania

Helen Susco is in her kitchen. As she goes about her work, she glances at her nine-month-old baby boy, sleeping in his cradle. She calculates how soon he will be awake and requiring her attention. Her oldest daughter, Ann, is rocking the baby's cradle next to the stove.

Suddenly there is a bang and a howling whoosh. "Ooh, hear dat wind, Annie?" Helen says.

The little girl turns to look out of the window. "Look at the trees bending, Mama!"

Helen joins her at the window in time to see the wild dance of trees and bushes accompanied by small cyclones of swirling leaves, papers, and other debris. A tin bucket skids across the alley and slams into a backyard shed. "Big storm gonna come. Where are de udder kids?"

Before Ann has a chance to answer, a long, deep roll of thunder sends a shudder through the house. Mother and daughter look to see if the noise has disturbed the baby, but he sleeps on.

Then they hear the fat drops of rain begin to pummel the porch roof, first hard and loud, then soft, then loud again, then louder still, as the sound is amplified by great, fearsome blasts of wind.

"I'm worried dat dem kids ain't..." Helen stops as angry lightning crackles against the dark purple bruise of sky, just visible through the kitchen window.

Helen likely saw the flash as it slammed into the stove, jumped over Ann and the baby, and knocked over a table. But no one ever really knew whether she caught the evil smell of ozone or felt the massive blow as the lightning struck her body or had any sense at all of hitting the floor.

———

Helen and John Susco immigrated to the United States from Russia during the great European influx as the twentieth century was just unfolding. Somewhere along the way the spelling of their name was changed from Sushko to the more American Susco. The Suscos settled in Western Pennsylvania in a town called Turtle Creek.

They knew nothing of the rich history of this bustling industrial center. This struggling young immigrant couple would have had no interest in the area's past as a lush and life-sustaining Indian hunting-ground, nor in its importance as a Revolutionary War-era tavern stop for covered wagons and stage coaches. And if they didn't know about George Washington and his famous dinner at the tavern in Turtle Creek, they probably knew only a little more about George Westinghouse whose brilliant inventions evolved into a world-renowned operation employing thousands of people and manufacturing products that revolutionized the world.

What the Suscos did know was that John could find work as a laborer in the Turtle Creek Valley alongside other Russian immigrants. So he and his young wife made their home there in a neighborhood where thousands of Eastern European families lived. In the valley that lies between the foothills of the Allegheny Mountains, just twelve miles from the city of Pittsburgh, the two started their family in modest comfort, surrounded by many of the sounds, smells, and tastes of the old country they had fled. First born was Nick, then Ann, then Kathryn, Mary, Helen, Johnny, and baby Michael. They attended the Russian Orthodox Church and, like most everyone else, struggled to pay the bills and feed the children.

The Suscos had made friends with a couple who lived in their hillside neighborhood. The Mauritzes were Roman Catholics who had emigrated from Austria-Hungary at about the same time that the Suscos had come to the United States.

Maybe it was the men who first met in one of the neighborhood taverns. After all, Frank Mauritz spoke four languages, including Russian. There could have been long talks between the Russian immigrant John Susco and Frank Mauritz on cold winter nights in the warm, noisy tavern.

"You got any kids, Frank?" John might have asked.

"My wife and me," Mauritz would have answered, " we had a child before we came here to this country. But the baby was weak and didn't live long. He's buried back in Sarajevo. Then my Antonia could never have another. And you, Susco?"

"Oh, we got six kids with another on the way. It's hard, you know, but God will provide."

Compared to the Susco family, the Mauritzes were financially comfortable. Frank, who would likely have qualified as a mechanical genius, was a highly valued tool and die man for Westinghouse. He had risen through the ranks to the position of group leader. He fit in well in his department, where German was the spoken language. Although it was not their native tongue, the Mauritzes always spoke German at home or when they needed to converse privately in their neighborhood, probably because few of their neighbors understood German.

It is possible that Frank and Antonia were warmed by the child-filled Susco household. Perhaps the Susco children helped to fill the emptiness the childless Antonia and Frank may have felt. Surely they had shown some affection to the older Susco children: when Michael was born, the Suscos asked Antonia and Frank Mauritz to be the baby's godparents, despite their religious differences.

When Helen Susco was struck by lightning, the force of it so damaged her brain and nervous system that it robbed her of her sanity. In legal documents she was described as having become a "lunatic with no lucid intervals." So the thirty-seven-year-old mother of seven was sent away to a state hospital for the mentally ill.

With little money for medical care and even less for raising his children, this father of seven had to make heart-wrenching decisions quickly. John Susco placed his six older children in an orphanage and asked his friends, Frank and Antonia Mauritz, to care for the baby, their godchild, Michael.

So the very storm that devastated the Suscos brought Antonia and Frank Mauritz sweet family life at last. How they must have yearned for another child after the loss of their baby in the old country! And here, finally, in their home, a home that was most likely too quiet, in their care was this baby boy.

Like moving from black and white to full, radiant color, the experience of living is changed by a child. Mere existence unfolds to reveal a more vibrant level of being when a baby comes into the lives of people who have been denied the gift of children. There is undoubtedly adjustment, turmoil, and even hardship when those unaccustomed to such demands find themselves sleep-deprived and utterly responsible for answering the needs of this wailing, drooling creature with a big wobbly head and a toothless smile. But what wonders are worked on the human heart when tiny fingers grasp yours and the baby face brightens at the sound of your voice and is soothed only at your touch! You are finally connected with the deeper, richer reaches of life. A child needs you. How completely and irrevocably you come to love him.

Those wounded hearts that had sadly hidden away their tenderest feelings upon the death of their baby were finally set free to feel again. And in the fullness of time, Antonia, Frank, and the child, Michael, became a family.

Who is to say that the bonds forged by this combination of need, choice, and desire aren't stronger than simple biology? As the poem written in the voice of a mother to her adopted baby says, "You grew not under my heart but in it." There are some things in the Lord's creation far greater than flesh and blood.

The baby was nurtured and grew strong in this loving family. And because Frank and Antonia primarily spoke German at home, little Michael, or *Mi' kit za* as Antonia called him, did so as well.

"*Bitta, Mama, bitta!*" little Michael would plead when he wanted a special treat. Antonia and Frank, after all, had become mother and father to the little boy. He knew no other parents, and the love the Mauritzes had for him was now deep and fixed. But before Michael would enter school and learn to speak proper English, the child himself would be forced to choose between families.

Nearly four years after lightning struck Helen Susco, she recovered her sanity and was released from the hospital in excellent health. Whether her sanity returned slowly after long therapy sessions or suddenly like a glorious resurrection, no one ever knew. But immediately upon her release the six older children were brought home from the orphanage and John and

Helen asked for the return of the now five-year-old Michael.

Although little is known of the actual exchanges that must have taken place over the custody of this child, the unending bitterness that stood between the two families for the remainder of their lives serves as testimony to the ferocity of the struggle.

Upon learning that the Suscos expected Michael to be returned to them, Frank and Antonia Mauritz petitioned the court of Allegheny County to legally adopt Michael Susco. How these two must have pleaded with the court not to take this child, the only child they would ever have, from the only parents he had ever known! And although there was surely an investigation of both families, with depositions taken and medical records reviewed in the usual manner, some crucial piece of evidence must have led the presiding judge to take the approach he did in rendering his decision. Like the wise King Solomon in the Bible, this judge resolved the conflict in this way: On an appointed day, at an appointed time, both of the mothers—Helen, the birth mother, and Antonia, the foster mother—were to be present in the courtroom. They were to stand in plain view on opposite sides of the room. The toddler would be brought into the room and allowed to go to whichever woman he chose. The judge explained that his decision would be based entirely upon the choice made by the child.

When Michael entered the courtroom on that day, he ran directly into the arms of Antonia Mauritz.

A Cherished Boy

Michael, no longer a Susco, enjoyed a childhood that was, for the Depression era, privileged. When many couldn't even afford bus fare, Michael's father, Frank, owned a car. And what a car! Michael would always remember that used 1923 Chevy as a symbol of his father's mechanical genius, because the elder Mauritz had taken the vehicle and turned the turtle-back into a pick-up truck! Young Michael would watch in awe each winter as his father, determined to make the Chevy run smoothly, took the entire engine apart, cleaned and repaired it meticulously, and rebuilt it. Here the old question of nature or nurture surfaces as young Michael began to show a remarkable mechanical ability, taking apart every toy he ever owned and, like his father, rebuilding it to perfection.

As the only child of a father who earned a comfortable living and a mother who poured all of her love and energy into the raising of her son, young Michael had it good indeed. On Sundays the Mauritz family would go to the Roman Catholic Church, where Michael received the holy sacraments. Michael, always a skinny, scrappy kid, would spend happy days playing baseball in neighboring fields or "Tin Can Alley" on the streets, or hurling himself into the swimming hole that he and the other boys had created when they dammed the chilly waters of the creek. Saturdays would find young Michael, now called Mickey by his friends, with a gang of kids at Turtle Creek's Olympic and Keystone Theaters. There he'd sit, thrilling to the adventures of cowboy heroes and Tarzan. Then, after a good dose of Hollywood, the boys would be off into the dense woods surrounding the town of Turtle Creek to build tree houses and reenact their favorite action-film stories.

When he was nine years old, Michael began spending long stretches of the summer on a farm that belonged to the Callus family, close friends of Frank and Antonia. The Calluses had two sons and a daughter, all near Michael's age. For all of his life Michael would remember as idyllic his summers in the green, rolling countryside near Mamont, Pennsylvania. He learned to do farm chores and gained a good sense of farm life. And his closeness with the Callus children gave him the experience of having siblings.

All the while he was growing up, Michael knew that the Suscos, who lived just about a block away, up the hill, were his birth family. He hadn't been told the circumstances of his adoption; all he knew was that there was bitterness between the two families, so Michael had no relationship with the Suscos. He had no special feeling for his birth parents; they were merely people his family once knew, people who happened to be his biological mother and father.

As a teen, he would sometimes give Helen Susco rides up the hill, as long as he was out of sight of his mother, Antonia. Once, while he was overseas in the service, he drew a pencil sketch of a girl he admired and, inexplicably, sent the drawing to his birth mother. The girl would one day be of great importance in his life, but Helen would never quite come into focus for the boy or for the man Michael would become.

At home, Michael always spoke German to his parents and they to him. Although they continued to dote on him, they also expected good behavior, good manners, and hard work. If he came home from school with paddle marks on the backs of his legs, he would get another whipping from his father for causing his teacher grief.

"Sonny!" Frank Mauritz called to his son one day.

"Yah, Papa?"

"I think it's good that you have been earning money carrying golf clubs at that fancy Edgewood Club. You started there when you were how old?"

"When I was ten."

"Well, you're thirteen now and it's time you learned a craft."

"But I like being a caddy. Now that I'm bigger, I'll make ninety cents a loop. And when I carry double, I can make more!"

"No, no, Sonny. You are going to be an apprentice at the Penn Cash Meat Market...you know, downstreet? I fixed it up for you. You will learn to be a butcher. First you will learn, then if you do good, they will pay you. You'll have to tell Edgewood you can't come anymore."

And so it was settled. At the age of thirteen, Michael Mauritz could be found at the Penn Cash Meat Market every day after school until six in the evening, and on Saturdays, starting at six in the morning. On those long workdays, Michael liked to take his lunch break at the White Tower Restaurant. His meal of two hamburgers, piece of pie, and cup of coffee would cost him twenty-five cents, but he thought it worth every penny. Eventually Michael became good enough at his work in the meat market to earn a six-dollar-a-week salary. Although the Mauritz family was doing well by Depression-era standards, Michael's six dollars a week was put to good use by Antonia.

When he wasn't in school or at the meat market, young Mauritz found time for the things he really loved. He had developed a keen interest in ham-radio operation. Like so many, particularly those in the Turtle Creek area where Westinghouse had given birth to KDKA, the first commercial radio station, young Mauritz was captivated by the big radio craze. He built his own crystal set and spent happy hours communicating with friends and neighbors over the airwaves. It was this passion for the radio that finally bridged the gap between Michael and his birth family, or at least one member of it. John Susco, the child closest to him in age, was also a radio buff, and it was through the crackling, breaking radio signal that Michael and John built a friendship that would last a lifetime. However, their friendship was never to mend the wound between the Mauritz and the Susco families, just as it would never take the two young men into brotherhood. Friends they were and friends they remained. And Michael was for all time the son of Antonia and Frank.

Michael Mauritz pleased his father when he chose the vocational track at Turtle Creek's Union High School. "Study hard and you'll get a good job," the ever-practical Frank Mauritz would say.

Michael excelled in work with electricity and was attracted to the sciences. His clear, logical mind grasped mathematics easily. He also enjoyed art, especially sketching. He had an "eye," they said. His easy-going manner and quiet wit earned him popularity, though his parents kept a tight rein on him.

His father had taught him to drive on a 1930 Pontiac. But even if Frank Mauritz had approved, Michael would have had little time to cruise around town with friends. Late afternoons during the school year, you would see the lanky figure of the young man dashing from school to his job at the meat market downtown. Then, taking long strides up the hill, the boy would head home to study and tinker in the garage out back where his father had taught him the fine art of automotive mechanics. Michael was still interested in ham radio, but now his focus had expanded to include shortwave.

Upon graduation in 1939, young Mauritz was offered another apprenticeship, this one at the great Westinghouse Corporation, in control-panel wiring. His parents were delighted. In those days and for decades afterward, Westinghouse was the center of the universe to many young men and women coming of age in Turtle Creek, Pennsylvania. Even in the greater Pittsburgh region and throughout southwestern Pennsylvania, a job at Westinghouse was something to attain. The electrical giant not only offered a lifetime of security to its workers, it gave them the opportunity to share in the magnificence of cutting-edge technology and world-wide recognition.

Just as he had in high school, Mauritz worked hard and caught on quickly at Westinghouse. He advanced from apprentice to specialist in control-panel wiring and secured an enviable future for himself. But it was not long after he completed his apprenticeship that young Mauritz began to consider what his parents would call the unthinkable.

News of the war had swarmed about him for years. Europe was collapsing. Mauritz became accustomed to seeing his father listening gravely to the radio broadcasts as country after country fell. The war was all the talk on the shortwave, in the halls at Westinghouse, and on the streets of Turtle Creek. Then, Pearl Harbor. The great fire had touched American soil and taken American lives. Young men all over the country felt the pull, the urge, to join. Although his work at Westinghouse gave him an automatic deferment, Mauritz begged his parents to allow him to enlist. Michael Mauritz knew that he had to be a part of this drama. Every instinct he possessed urged him toward this war, which represented a clear struggle between good and evil. He had grown up fed by such struggles, watching those classic battles in the movie houses every Saturday morning. He had thrived on it, enacting the scripts, playing in the woods behind his house, aping the heroes. Now he wanted to live it, because he had to live it. Michael was part of that singular generation, that unique group who, without knowing it, would be among the last Americans of the century, of the millennium, to have no reason to doubt their duty. Right stood on one side, tall and strong, square-jawed with clenched fists, while wretched evil loomed hideously on the other. This war was a fight you just had to get into…if you had any stuff in you at all.

Michael knew there were some who might gratefully cling to their deferments. But he could not be one of those. He was sickened by the thought of himself at the end of this war, untouched and unscathed, still clinging to his coveted Westinghouse position. How could he face the returning soldiers? He knew that anything short of direct involvement in the war effort would diminish and perhaps even ruin him.

"Why should we sign for you to maybe get hurt or killed?" his father would say. "No, you have a good job at the company, a good future, and you're doing your part for the war. What more do you want?"

And from his mother, "*Bitta*, Sonny. We're so lucky you don't have to go! You can't trow dat away! Too many have been kilt already!"

His dream was to be in the Air Corps, to fly! He was so captivated by the idea that he had even taken a few private lessons in secret. And now flying was his dream and fighting for his country, his obsession.

By May of 1942, Michael was twenty-one years old and free to enter this war that would become the defining event for his generation. Now he would shed his hated deferment and give himself to this moment in history. Shortly after his birthday, Mauritz went downtown to Pittsburgh and took tests for the Air Corps to become an aviation cadet.

He passed the mental tests handily, but there was one problem. "Come back in a month, son, after you've gained some weight."

So the boy who preferred tinkering with a car engine to coming in for dinner now devoted himself to milkshakes and banana splits, noodles, dumplings, and warm buttered bread.

"Frank, our boy eats now so much just so he can go over der to a war he doesn't even have to fight."

"He's not a boy anymore."

With his gift for numbers and science and his considerable mechanical talents, Michael qualified easily for the elite Army Air Corps Cadets. But he would have to wait two months until a new class was scheduled to begin. It wouldn't work. Michael Mauritz had already given himself over to this war; he had, in every important way, left his old life behind. Waiting wasn't possible for him. Friends were gone now. His parents were so sad. Still, the war was compelling. So he did what he had to do: he enlisted and went off to basic training with the other volunteers and those who had been drafted.

A Part of It All
From the Journal of Michael Mauritz

9/11/42, Fort Meade, Maryland

Settled in now. Glad I left. It's good to be here. I'm sorry about Mom and Pop but it feels right here even though I'm sort of the odd duck in this group. What a combination of guys! They're from everywhere—places I never even heard of. Some of these men are pretty miserable about being here. There's a lot of drinking going on and sometimes when a fellow has had too much he gets to crying about this place or his girl at home or getting killed or something. Some of them are pretty broken up over being here and I guess some are just homesick. I think those summers I spent on the farm away from Mom and Pop helped me to grow up and be able to do this. Funny, but I think I was being prepared for this and just didn't know it.

They cut all my hair off but I kind of like it.

9/13/42, Fort Meade, Maryland

Basic is just like I thought it would be. But not so awful as some say. A few of the guys are getting so drunk they come in and crawl into the first bunk they can find...even if there's someone else in it! Most are smart enough to just get up and find another bunk. Some, though, just go off like crazy people, pounding the poor sap who's had too much. You see it all here...compassion, brutality, acceptance...everything. I figured out that in order to get through this and serve the way you should, you have to hold yourself together. It's hard to explain exactly but it's like you just can't let yourself fly off the handle or even open up too much to anyone. You need to stay calm and relaxed deep inside, just like Pop. Try to do things like you always did. For me, if I sit quietly and sketch a while or read a good western, I can kind of pull myself back into a sort of peaceful place where I know I'm okay. I don't really need anyone around me but at the same time, no one is bothering me or getting on my nerves. I can just get along with everyone and accept each one for what he is.

We're off to Miami Beach soon. Sounds better than it actually is, I'm sure.

10/3/42, Miami Beach, Florida

It is damn hot here! We're staying in a pretty swell beach hotel but it's no vacation. I spent the first night alone. Did some sketching and reading, got some rest. But on the second night I got a buddy. And what a story he had! It seems his roommate for the first night wanted to get romantic with him! He says it was some shocking experience. He couldn't get out of there fast enough.

I asked him what happened to the guy.

"Well," he said, "when I told him nothing doing, he was pretty embarrassed. I almost felt sorry for him. So I just left and requested another room. I didn't want to make trouble for him or anything. After all, he backed off right away."

I admired him for that. Not making trouble. I don't understand that stuff but I can't see hurting a guy for being that way. Just let it go. There are more important things to fight about.

I'll be leaving for training in San Antonio soon. They call it "SAACC." Get it? San Antonio Aviation Cadet Center. I am no longer Private Mauritz, because I'm now officially an aviation cadet, so they're calling me either Cadet or Mister. Sounds good to me! I understand I'll be tested for classification. Could end up as a navigator, tail gunner or bombardier. But at least I'll be flying. Here's hoping!

11/20/42, San Antonio, Texas

Got a nice box from home...most of it grub (I liked that) and some new westerns to read. Not exactly Thanksgiving dinner but it will do. The testing here is tough. A lot of psycho-motor-skill stuff to tell how ambidextrous you are. I can see how important that would be for a fighter pilot. Some of it is very difficult. I am holding on, though. I guess I'll end up doing what I'm supposed to do and that will be fine.

The upperclassmen get all the breaks here. They're served first at meals...things like that. Besides the classification testing, their job here is to make us into gentlemen. That means looking good all of the time, being clean (some guys who don't shower often enough get tossed into the showers) and using your best manners at the table. Things like cutting your bread into fours and buttering it one piece at a time or sitting up straight at dinner, bringing the food to your mouth and not "dive bombing," as they call it, and shoveling it in. If you get caught doing that, you have to eat a square meal. Now that's a pain!

The hazing is kind of silly, stuff like asking the water fountain, "Mr. Fountain, may I have a drink?" But it all finally works toward smoothing us out and making us into officers and gentlemen and good flyers, too. One of the things we have to do when we're out walking and come to a crosswalk is look both ways before proceeding, like it was a street or something. The purpose is for us as future flyers to become accustomed to constantly looking around us when turning in a new direction.

Looking around for danger, the enemy.

I got off easy the other day when I showed up for dinner. I could see some of the upperclassmen looking at me and laughing and it took me a while to figure out what was going on. I had forgotten my tie! But they didn't do anything to me. They just let me slide. I did better than Rosen. He's Jewish and some of the guys don't like him just for that. I don't get it. He's a good guy, a regular guy, and a good friend. But these upperclassmen wanted to get him, so they took his bedsprings and hung them from a balcony. It was stupid. They made it look like good fun, you know, like hazing. But everyone knew what it was really all about. They don't like his being Jewish. They don't want a Jew around. It was shameful what they did. Hard to believe some of these men who are supposed to be officers and gentlemen have that kind of hate in them. Stupid!

1/14/43, San Antonio, Texas

Made it! Made it! Made it! I'm a flyer! I'm very grateful. I have a long way to go yet, but it's good and I love it. I made it!

1/20/43, Muskogee, Oklahoma

The training is fascinating. Going up there is something! Mr. Cooper, a flight trainer, takes you up in a PT-19. He sits in front, you in back, strapped in. Then he rolls the plane (upside down) and says, "Show me your hands!" He screams! No kidding! *Show me your hands!* So there you are, hanging, and you have to let go and put your arms straight up. He takes you through snap rolls. That's when you pull back and go into this horizontal spin with a quick recovery. Then he cuts the throttle and yells, "Force landing!" and you have to take over and try to find a place where you can put the plane down safely, then institute what they call a "dead-stick landing." I'm doing okay with it. I try to think my way through and just concentrate on what I know and not on what could go wrong.

Did I mention how much Mr. Cooper screams all of the time, every minute that you're trying to fly the damn plane? And I don't mean just cussing. I mean he tries to get to you with sort of personal stuff, like "You stupid jerk! You are really a fool! Everyone thinks so! They all think you're a joke! You don't belong here!" Things like that, and then if you make a mistake he whacks you with the plane's stick. No kidding. One guy got so upset with Mr. Cooper that when they landed he chased Cooper saying he was going to beat the hell out of him for making him so nervous while they were flying. But I think that's just what he's trying to teach you. You gotta learn to take it and still concentrate on what you're doing. You're flying the plane and nothing and no one should rattle you. You have to remember what you know, think about what you have to do, and do it! You are the pilot. Period. Pop would love it here!

2/6/43, Muskogee, Oklahoma

I'm swamped with classroom work and study. I enjoy the time I'm flying and I feel comfortable up there. By the way, the food here is wonderful!

2/10/43, Muskogee, Oklahoma

I soloed today. I did it!!! I was nervous but I just kept thinking about what I know—you know, focusing on what I was taught. It went fine. Once I was into it I was calm and it was easy. I kept thinking about Pop. The way he always concentrates on things he's doing and just shuts everything else out. He would like knowing that he taught me to do that. I'm very far away from him and everything at home now. It's better that way.

There was one poor guy who was soloing but he froze when it was time to land. He'd come in short and pull up, then come in too long. It went on and on. Someone said, "Maybe they'll have to shoot the poor bastard down." But finally an instructor flew alongside and helped him land. I thought maybe they'd wash him out but they didn't. They just kept working with him and he did it eventually. He could have done it all along.

3/22/43, Independence, Kansas

Independence Army Flying School. This is some place! We entered on buses coming under a big sign that read "Through these gates pass the best damn students in the world!" This is where we really learn to be pilots and officers. They make you feel good here because you know they think you're pretty smart to have made it this far. And they keep telling us that the training we get here is equal to none. And they're teaching us to fly the fastest planes on earth! The feeling is like nothing else I've ever experienced.

After reading what I just wrote, I see that I've bought the program lock, stock, and barrel. All that "go go, can do" attitude. I know a lot of it is a sell job, but a lot of it is true and they have to keep morale high. How the hell else can we go over there and do the job?

The thing is that here is where we have learned to become military. Back in Oklahoma, it was flying. Now, Independence is advanced flying, but it's flying in the MILITARY!

4/18/43, Independence, Kansas

It's a beautiful spring here. Even more beautiful up there. It always is. But now we're working on flying blind. Learning the instruments using the Link Trainer. They put you under the hood and you learn to do everything without taking your eyes off the instruments. You have to leave your instincts behind. It's all counter to almost everything you ever learned—not trusting your gut, just your brain. When you're up in poor visibility, you can't tell up from down or sideways even. You have to trust your instruments. Trust, trust, trust.

All this gentleman crap we're learning even includes learning to drink like gentlemen! I didn't really know anything about drinking, so one night when we went out I asked my friend Ross, "What are you supposed to drink?" He suggested a Cuba Libre. It's rum and coke with a slice of lime. Cuba Libre, it means "Free Cuba!" Well, I freed Cuba all night and then my stomach revolted. Was I sick!

4/20/43, Independence, Kansas

We've been working on night landings, flying BT-14's. I felt confident about landing at night but every time I tried it, I could feel my trainer moving the controls instead of letting me do it. I figured he didn't trust me and I might never get a chance to solo at night. So I decided to go over his head. I told the check pilot what was happening and asked if he'd take me up. When he did, he just let me go on and fly. When we got up he was busy yelling at everyone else flying around us in the pattern, shouting instructions to them. So I went ahead and landed the plane and when we got out he kind of laughed at me and said, "Go ahead and kill yourself." But I didn't and now I made it. So I'm certified to solo and land at night. One more step!

I'm not exactly considered to be one of the roughest, toughest guys in the outfit (ha ha, no kidding) but because I don't mix it up, maybe some guys wondered about my doing this (side-stepping the trainer). Well, it's like I know what I know and I'm not afraid to stand up for myself when it's like that. It was just so clear to me that I had to take care of things myself. I wasn't out to get the trainer. I wasn't even mad at him. No anger, none at all. I'm sure of that. I just knew I could do it, and I couldn't sit around and let the guy hold me back. I had to move on. I knew I could and that's all there is to it.

6/6/43, Victoria, Texas

We're flying AT-6's now, the most famous trainer in the world. There I go again with that *Life Magazine* stuff! This is advanced training and what we have to do is keep it straight and level—straight and level, because now the shooting begins. We'll be off soon to a place called Matagorda Island. One more step.

6/8/43, Matagorda Island, Texas

This is the most desolate spot I've ever seen! I've been sketching it but I don't know if I can quite get the absolute nothingness of this place. We're here to learn fixed guns (one machine gun on the AT-6 trainer).

The training is interesting. They have a plane towing a target that's about twenty feet across. Then we come by and make what is called a "pursuit pass"...and you have to aim ahead of your target and I think the instructors have some bets going on their students. There may even be a little cheating going on among the trainers in this competition to see whose team is hitting the target the most.

As I was unpacking my stuff at the BOQ, I opened a drawer and found it filled with cockroaches! So I found myself a rope and hung my barracks bag from the ceiling. Welcome to Matagorda!

7/24/43, Victoria, Texas

I am officially an officer now. We had an impressive graduation ceremony. When I think about writing about it, I don't know if I can accurately convey the power of it—the marching bands and flags flying under the clear blue Texas sky. It was moving—the troops assembled in dress uniform. And the speeches—they told us we were the best, the best in the world. Best trained, best educated, best fed. And they told us to remember that we were the best.

8/4/43, Sarasota, Florida

It's hot as hell here—a jungle kind of heat. More training, this time replacement fighter training in P-40's. We are learning combat formation here, and practicing dive-bombing along with low-level cross-country flights. I love it.

9/25/43, Camp Patrick Henry, Virginia

I was assigned to read outgoing mail for censorship. One letter read, "I can't tell you where I am but *Give me liberty or give me death!*" Pretty clever! Ha Ha. We're shipping out soon. This is it, but I feel ready. It will be okay.

Into the Fray

10/2/43, Somewhere in the Atlantic aboard an ocean liner converted into a troop carrier

We were supposed to have staterooms. But some higher-ranking Red Cross gals bumped us and we're sleeping in hammocks, if you please! We're crossing unescorted. They say it's because this ship is so fast it could outrun enemy subs. Let's hope so.

The Atlantic is beautiful. It's moody and fickle, a different color every day. Blue, green, gray, darker gray. Some people are having problems with seasickness but not too many. Most of us have taken to this pretty well. I think the worst of it at first was the noise of the engines at night. But once you get used to it, it's no problem at all. I just can't get over the size of the sky out here. When you look at the horizon, you can really understand why people once thought they would fall off the end of the earth if they sailed too far. Best of all is the sky at night when you're at sea. There are so many more stars than I ever thought there were! I like to stare up at the constellations, just like I did as a kid, lying in the backyard. I wonder how it can all look just the same with the world in such turmoil, with all the destruction and death. When I think about the beauty of that big, starlit, black canopy over us at sea, it's hard to imagine that we're even on our way to a war.

My job is below deck. I am assigned to guard the troops. That means that in the event of an emergency I have to sit on the steps that lead topside and keep the men below deck, using my weapon if necessary. I would never want to have to do that—not to our own, not to anyone if I could choose. But I would do what I have to do because I know how important it is to maintain order and calm in an emergency. Many more could be hurt or killed if you don't keep things under control.

I'll try to make time for sketching later today if there is any light left.

10/21/43, Casablanca, Morocco

Everything here is intense. The colors are solid, blank, and singular. The blue of the sky, the green sea, the white buildings, and the heat…like a Pittsburgh blast furnace. Then the sun sets, and bang! You'd think a huge door was slammed shut. I mean, you freeze your ass off!

Military everywhere in this city. Our bunks are metal straps with thin mattresses on them. A few of us went down to the Casbah last night. It's a wild place…strange sights, sounds, and even stranger smells. Later we were told that the Casbah was off limits to military personnel. You could definitely get into big trouble down there. I heard about some guys who lost all their money, got beat-up, robbed, or ended up sick as dogs. My thinking is that overseas you have to keep yourself under control. You've got to hold it all together 'cause if you start going crazy over one thing or another—like gambling, drink, women, or fighting—you could go all the way and just crumble to bits. I think the guys who will make it are the ones who hold on tight. Stay calm and quiet, try to get along with everyone and keep cool. I usually do pretty well at this, but one little adventure that seemed safe enough nearly led us to tragedy.

We were told there was a large quantity of c-rations just left in a warehouse here, and my friend Wally and I thought we should liberate them for the train ride we were going to be taking. Well, on the way over to the warehouse we had to cross a railroad yard. While we were ducking between two freight cars, one of them started to move backward and just missed crushing us by inches. The Lord was with us in that moment. We each managed to carry a box of over forty cans back with us.

10/29/43, Crossing the desert

We've been on this train for three days now and probably have another two or so to go. We're riding in what they call a forty-and-eight—so named because this car can hold forty men and eight horses! I'm glad we're doing without the damn horses. We all smell bad enough. We sleep and eat in our seats…if you can call it eating.

We talk some about our lives and our experiences in training. We talk sports and a little bit about home and girls. After a time, I like to be quiet and read. I've been doing a lot of sketching. I'd like to stop long enough to sketch some of the people–their weathered skin, the billowing robes they wear—they must look like people did in biblical times. I was looking out of the window a little while ago and I was fascinated watching this man riding on a burro. The creature was so small that the man's feet were almost dragging on the ground. Trailing behind him in a line were his wives carrying all of his belongings! Some country!

This afternoon the train was going so slowly up a mountain that we got out and walked alongside. The exercise felt good. There were people along the way but we had to keep up with the train. I've never seen such blue skies. And the light here is sharp and hard. But the heat! It's so dry it can really get you before you know it. It's so different from the humid summer heat of home. We all need showers. This train stinks like hell.

12/11/43, North Africa

First flight in a P-40. We have to get our flying time in (at least four hours to qualify for flight pay, which is half of our base pay).

The British are setting up a radio homing system here, so we have been asked to give them practice on our local training flights.

12/24/43, North Africa

Busy flying missions now. It doesn't seem at all like Christmas. We're trying hard to make the best of things.

Italy

At the start of 1944, Lieutenant Michael Mauritz and a group of fighter pilots were ordered from North Africa to Foggia, Italy, where they were assigned to the 86th Fighter Squadron of the 79th Fighter Group, comprised of the 85th, 86th, 87th, and 99th, camped at Termoli. The 99th was a segregated group consisting of the famous Tuskegee Airmen. These were the African Americans who were trained to fly combat at the 66th Air Force Flying School at the Tuskegee Institute in Tuskegee, Alabama. The Tuskegee Airmen would forever change the relationship between the U. S. military establishment and African-American service men and women. But their struggle was great. Even though they had set high standards for themselves and succeeded brilliantly, their triumphs weren't always recognized. It was not until the end of the war that their skill and bravery did finally bring about integration of the Air Force. Even though they returned to a still-segregated country, history could hardly ignore the importance of these legendary aviators who never lost an aircraft during battle. Michael Mauritz and many of the others in the 79th would always be proud to have served alongside the legendary Tuskegee Airmen.

Mauritz and the others assigned to the 86th were slated to fly Curtiss P-40L's. Although this plane was, at the time, considered out of date, it was still rated as a formidable fighter-bomber due to its capacity to drop one-thousand-pound loads while diving. Nothing came close to the P-40L Warhawk until the introduction of the P-47 Thunderbolt and the P-51 Mustang.

While Mauritz and his comrades were stationed at

Termoli, the young lieutenant executed five combat missions. Three of the missions involved dive-bombing and strafing. On a fifth mission, Mauritz and his comrades were ordered to search for anti-aircraft guns. These missions took place one week before the great Allied landing at Anzio. Their purpose was to enable rapid air-cover deployment to the all-important bridgehead at Anzio.

The Allied invasion of Anzio on January 22, 1944, was intended to attack the rear of the German's right flank. At first, the Germans reeled from the masterful Allied surprise and the beachhead was firmly established. But once the Germans regrouped and poured in reinforcements, their resistance was powerful. It would take the Allies four months, often battling in foul winter weather, to permanently secure the Anzio beachhead. In the end, it would be explained that the importance of the hard-fought, bloody Battle of Anzio was that it diverted German troops from the main Allied offensive on the Italian peninsula. Experts claim that the Anzio operation contributed heavily to the initiative that resulted in the fall of Rome in May of 1944.

Immediately following the Anzio invasion, Mauritz and the 79th Fighter Group were moved to Naples. There the pilots were housed in an ancient and empty hotel outfitted only with sleeping bags. They were told they had to report every morning to Capodichino several miles away, using whatever means of transportation was available.

From the Journal of Michael Mauritz

1/28/44, Naples, Italy
I have to keep reminding myself that this is Italy. Look

what a brutal war can do! Everywhere, this beautiful country is grim, broken, and overrun. All those muddy footprints: ours and the Germans...the Fascists, too. Too many footprints. And now they've hardened in the January cold. There is a very different feeling here from North Africa with its big, flat, empty spaces. There weren't so many ugly scars there. But Italy is really showing her battle wounds and her battle fatigue. It's like looking at a poor, sick, old lady who was once very beautiful and elegant. There is so much decay and filth in Naples. Everything is crumbling! I saw a cemetery where bombs hit the above-ground vaults. It was horrible, they were split right open—not just the vaults but the caskets too, exposing the bodies. What a terrible sight.

Still, you can tell what a captivating place this must have been. The city sits at the base and kind of runs up the slopes of these hills that form a semicircle around the Bay of Naples. Mount Vesuvius just looms over the bay! (Some of the guys laugh at me and call me "Geography Book" because I like to pay attention to all that stuff. I think some of them hardly know what country they're in!) Anyway, Vesuvius is a live volcano and it once erupted and killed the entire village of Pompei, and now everything and everyone is entombed in the lava. I read about that but I don't like to think about it too much. I'm having a tough enough time getting those split-open caskets out of my mind. Even looking at the living Neopolitans is bad enough. Their grim faces. My image of Italy and the Italians was so different before this. These people are hungry and cold and tired—tired of this muddy war.

The hotel where we live was once a resort hotel when Italy was the Italy of romantic stories. When we all go to chow, we eat in a room on the main floor of the hotel. Outside, they set up barrels of soapy water and rinse water so that we can clean up after ourselves. Although they are kept at a distance, there is always a crowd of Neopolitans, mostly hungry, skinny, dirty kids watching and waiting for any leftovers or scraps we might have. Now that we know they will be there, we all try to leave something for them, and the kids dart across the street to gratefully snatch whatever leftovers we can give them. I wish we had more to give.

I have had some good luck. As soon as we got here, we were all a little worried about having to find our own way up to the airfield at Capodichino. It's not all that close and we have to be there every morning. But almost immediately we met a sergeant who was selling his British-made BSA motorcycle for fifty bucks! It seems the poor guy had fallen on hard times and needed the money. Probably to pay his gambling debts. We don't know how he came by the motorcycle. All kinds of vehicles, ours and everyone else's, seem to be appropriated in a lot of, well, let's say, different ways. Anyway, two of us went together and bought the thing. After a little tinkering, I got her going pretty good and now, hell, we make it up to the airfield in no time!

Speaking of appropriated vehicles, a rumor went around, just after we bought our motorcycle, that a British lieutenant was investigating in the area, looking for "mis-appropriated" British transportation equipment. So we took our motorcycle and stood it up on end in a broom closet inside the hotel. We figured the lieutenant would never think to look there for his missing equipment.

The Last Day

1/22/99, Turtle Creek, Pennsylvania

I'm not so young anymore but I'm going to try to reconstruct events beginning with the day *Skipper* went down.

It was January 31, 1944. We made our way up to Capodichino on our motorcycle, thoroughly enjoying the ride on that cloudy but unusually mild morning. The twisted roads took us higher and higher in a thrilling spiral, and the wind whipping around us as we climbed added to the pleasure of the ride.

Once at the air base, we went straight to our morning briefing but were told there were no scheduled missions for us that day as another squadron was to fly that morning.

"Great!" I thought. "It's warm enough for me to get some work done on the motorcycle."

Our forces had landed at Anzio only a little more than a week earlier. The battle was fierce and our losses were heavy. We were told that German resistance was much greater than expected. So it looked like Anzio would drag on. Intelligence claimed the enemy was quickly building strength. Talk was that the Allies were going to be in for it.

But on this morning, I could push the war out of my mind for a little while and concentrate on getting that motorcycle in better shape. My father had given me my love of tinkering with engines, and I could always lose myself in the task. But I had hardly begun when a counter-order came in: there was a mission for the 86th, with immediate take-off!

49

I had to clean myself off pretty quickly and then head over to the plane they assigned me. It was a P-40L, #49, name of *Skipper*. It was usually assigned to an Edward E. Parsons, who had his name stenciled outside the cockpit. Today *Skipper* would be mine.

After undergoing a quick checkup, the twelve of us were off, in formation, heading for Anzio, flying cover for the ground troops. As we took off, the cloud cover was 10/10 with poor visibility, but Anzio was just a short hop to the northwest, up the coast from Naples. So I had no serious concerns until I got into the air. Then I noticed that instead of decreasing, as it's supposed to do, my engine temperature was increasing and doing so very quickly. I was puzzled. When it exceeded 150 degrees centigrade, I radioed Major Nielsen, our squadron leader, and reported my condition. He told me to stay with it since Anzio was only a few minutes away. He informed me there was a runway there where I could land. I was okay with that and initially thought that's what I would be doing. But when I looked again, I'll be damned if the temperature wasn't going right through the roof, faster than before!

I radioed again that I couldn't continue. I told Nielsen that I would have to attempt a landing at sea! Once I made that decision and actually said the words "landing at sea," everything started to come to me as clear and precise as could be—everything that I had been taught, everything that I needed to do, as if it were being fed to me. I responded in an incredibly calm and deliberate manner. First, I ditched my reserve fuel and lowered the landing flaps. Then I went into a 180-degree turn so that I could get myself parallel with the coast in a southern direction. When you're flying over water, it's difficult to determine your altitude unless you can get the shoreline in your peripheral vision. I did it with ease.

My calm continued, and everything that I needed to know came to me in a methodical and measured way, sort of like slow motion. I could feel myself breathing, but not hard as though I was scared or anything—just very deliberate, steady and sure. I opened the cockpit and prayed to lose altitude slowly. I wasn't frightened or particularly nervous, but I was concerned about that big radiator under the nose of my Warhawk with the air scoops—the very scoops that were supposed to be cooling my engine! If they hit the water first, the scoops would fill instantly and the plane would roll over, for sure—and I mean, a tail-over-nose cartwheel! I just prayed, "Oh God! Oh God!"

I did not think about drowning or being hurt. I simply knew it was vital for me to calibrate my descent correctly and make sure my tail touched down first. I was not a very religious man at that time, but what they say is true: there are no atheists in foxholes. Now, I was no atheist, but in those days I had not yet come to know the Lord. I guess you could say I didn't talk to Him much, but now I realize that He knew me. I believe He took a hand, especially as I came down lower and saw how calm and flat the sea was. If the sea had been choppy, that, too, could have caused the plane to cartwheel. "Thank God!" I kept saying, "Thank God!"

It was all slow and easy, as if my life had gone into slow motion or I was dreaming. I wasn't sensing anything bad. I was very calm. The beach on my left was in my periphery and I was able to use it a reference point of altitude. All that intense training paid off pretty good now and *Skipper* came down perfectly, tail first with its big old nose in the air. Again, thank God!

I maintained control of the plane, keeping that nose up

the whole time and leaving a nice wake behind me. The nose lowered itself into the water. Again my prayers were answered, because the only thing I felt was the abrupt stop—like hitting a wall— when the scoops finally hit the water. Not crashing into a wall, just hitting it. Believe me, there's a difference. And, of course, there was no rollover! I had done it: a successful dead-stick landing! (I say *I* had done it, but now I know how much help I had.)

I was so grateful to realize that that wonderful little P-40 floated perfectly even though it was taking on water. It was giving me enough time to get myself out of the cockpit and remove my shoulder straps and safety belt. I did get a little nervous when my parachute seemed to catch in the seat. The chute contained my survival kit. Well, to hell with the chute, I thought. I unharnessed myself to get free of it and managed to get out of the plane on the left wing. Now I was in the water, letting the Mae West float me, on my chest, the one hundred or so meters to shore. The water was cold but not unbearable. I was doing fine. I was okay.

As soon as I was in the water, *Skipper*'s nose began to sink as its tail rose. And as I watched, the chute suddenly freed itself! It was a final gift from *Skipper* before it would disappear under the sea. I swam back toward the plane, which was already half under water, caught hold of the strap, and pulled the chute toward me. Now I concentrated on getting to shore, pulling the chute after me. Again I let the Mae West float me in. I was not aware of being cold or anything. I just wanted to get under cover as fast as I could.

When I put my leg down to test for depth, I felt solid earth, so I sort of stood up and quickly got myself out of the water and onto the beach. One look back and I saw that *Skipper* had vanished under the sea. It was gone! I couldn't really think about it now. I saw some thick brush along the beach. First, I hid my parachute under one bush, then I stayed low and crawled like a crab a short distance into a row of bushes. I hoped that crawling would obscure the footprints my boots had made when I came out of the water.

Now my heart was pounding hard and I was thinking, "Okay, you're down. What now?" Off in the distance I could hear the drone of a plane...circling overhead. I thought it was most likely my squadron leader. As he made a pass, I saw something fall from the sky. I rushed forward and found a note saying that Anzio had been contacted and a rescue boat would be sent for me.

"I'm in good shape," I thought, and again, "Thank God!" Once I returned to the safety of the bushes, I could feel the cold. I was wet and shivering but I could still hear that plane. I removed my Mae West and thought, "They'll come for me now. I'll get out of here fast. It will just be a little while. He's radioed for help. Help will come. I'll just watch the sea and run for it the minute I see the launch." I imagined how good it would feel to be in the launch. I just kept playing that through my head while I shook with cold. It wasn't all that bad, because I was focused on watching for the launch. And that droning sound of the plane was a great comfort. I lay on my belly under the brush and positioned myself so that I could look out to sea. I figured the minute I saw the rescue launch, I'd make a run for it. Really run! I was in good shape. I could see out but no one could see me. I had every reason to believe that help was on the way. I was in good shape. I was getting out.

"*Hande hoch!*" (Hands up!)

I twisted around when I heard that voice and saw the

outline of a square helmet.

"Hande hoch !" More insistent and angry now.

"Aw, shit!" I thought.

When he leaned forward and extended his rifle barrel closer to me, I could see that he was young and boyish. Younger than me. It's so strange how in moments of extreme tension, you can actually be thinking something like, "Oh, this German soldier is just a kid," while fully realizing that this "kid" is the enemy and might just kill you.

I tried to get up on my hands and knees to crawl out toward him, but he shouted again, *"Hande hoch!"* So I put my hands up and struggled out on my knees from under the bushes. I no longer heard the plane above. I remember thinking, "Where in the hell is the plane?" As I cleared the bushes and stood, I saw two other German soldiers. They were each positioned on one knee, pointing their rifles at me from about ten feet away.

"Haben Sie ein Gewehr?" the young soldier barked.

"Nein, ich habe kein Gewehr," I answered. No, I do not have a gun.

Then in a more conversational tone, the young soldier explained in German, "We would have shot you if you had a gun."

Perhaps they would have shot me if they simply *thought* I had a gun. My young captor's expression had relaxed immediately when I answered him in German. At the same time the two others approached. Clearly my German had eased the tensions all around. Dear God, it may have saved my life! They were ready to shoot me, and my words, my German words, a gift from my parents, had made me less of a threat, I guess, more of a human being.

The best part of it was that answering him in German was a reflex. Someone spoke to me in German and so I answered in German without consciously doing so.

With a gesture of his rifle, my captor indicated the direction in which we were to proceed on foot, followed by the other two. We walked just a short distance to a house along the beach. I can't remember thinking much of anything at that point. I believe I was in a dream-like state, just acting mechanically. I was doing what they told me to do and that was enough. When I entered the house, a soldier handed me a blanket and allowed me to stand by a fire to warm myself. Now I realized the discomfort of being cold and wet and I was grateful for the blanket and the fire. It also occurred to me that I was being treated in a very civilized manner. But I told myself, "You're still a prisoner. You are behind lines and you are a prisoner."

I also knew that I had to think and decide what I could do, but I couldn't let myself think too much just yet. I had to get my thoughts together first and be careful how I acted toward my captors. Or maybe it was more that I had to test my strength—my spiritual strength, that is. I wasn't feeling frightened exactly. Anyway, I quickly reviewed what I knew I could bear to think about. Maybe I could use my German to my advantage. That was a good thing. I knew I had to escape, but I didn't know if an escape attempt was a good thing or a bad thing yet. I just knew that I could not let them take me to Germany. I knew that's what they would do and I couldn't let that happen. That was harder to think about just then, but I let it enter my mind in a conscious way and sit there. I had to escape and I would find a way. And that's all.

After a few minutes I was again ordered to follow my captors to their command post about two miles from the house, more or less in the same neighborhood. Along the way, I saw German troops in foxholes. "My God," I thought, "this is what a war is like." I wasn't used to seeing it from ground level. Even back in Naples, I had seen the effects of war but now I was witnessing it in the present tense. The privileged view from a plane surely has its dangers; still, it isolates you from the true sense of war—the flesh and blood of it, the smell of it, and the tiny details of it that put it on a human scale.

During the walk, in a moment when no one could hear or see, the young soldier who had captured me showed me the escape kit he had found in my parachute. Along with other items like a compass and a silk handkerchief with a map of Italy on it, the kit contained about forty American dollars. The soldier asked me not to tell his commanding officer about it. As he was speaking to me, I heard the sound of gunfire coming from the beach and figured it had something to do with the rescue launch sent for me. I felt hope rise up in me like a great warmth.

"The Navy, my comrades, is sending a rescue boat for me. I'll give you the money if you let me go right now to meet the rescue team," I offered in German.

"*Nein!*" he said, explaining that too many people had already seen me. His allowing me to escape could get him killed.

I told him to keep the money and promised to tell no one. He could have killed me and didn't. This kid, who should be at home, still in high school chasing girls, had probably had a tough time of it. That forty dollars might just buy him some little bit of comfort or fun.

We continued on to the German command post. I heard no more planes, no more gunfire. I felt desolate. I tried not to think. I would hold myself together. I would think later.

Inside the command post we were met by an immaculately dressed lieutenant who took the escape kit. I was then led to a room where their commanding officer was seated at a desk. He directed me to sit in the chair opposite his desk and, pointing to a bottle of liquor in his desk, offered me a drink. I refused politely, answering him in German.

Showing no surprise that I spoke his language, he asked cordially, "You fly a P-40?"

"Yes, I do," I answered.

"Tell me, what do you think of the P-40 compared to the 109?"

I admitted that the 109 was a better aircraft. "But," I added, "the U. S. had the P-40 in production at the time we entered the war."

I was shaking with cold as I watched the officer pour himself a drink. I realized that the warmth of the liquor was just what I needed. "I would like to accept your offer and have that drink with you," I said in German.

He poured me a drink and I gulped it gratefully. "*Danka*," was all I said.

Abruptly, but still with rather good humor, the officer called for the lieutenant who had escorted me in. I was still carrying the army blanket the Germans had given me earlier as we walked back into the outer office. As soon as the door to the commander's office was closed, the lieutenant ordered me to remove my leather flying jacket.

"My jacket? It's getting awfully cold out there," I said in German, keeping my voice as neutral as possible. Ever since I was a kid I knew that you never let a bully see emotion.

"Give me the jacket," he answered slowly and quietly. "That blanket is good enough." There was no mistaking his tone. I removed my jacket and handed it over to him. Without a word, he took it from me. When he had it in his hands, he shoved me through the door where two German soldiers were waiting on a motorcycle. Just then, the thought of my motorcycle back at Capodichino made me feel hopeless. I had to force the thought of Capodichino and Naples from my mind. As a pilot I had grown accustomed to coming back after a mission. Back to a bed, a shower, hot food. I knew we were luckier than most. Again I thought what life must be like in a war down on the ground, living in a foxhole. Now *I* was down, cold and wet. I was a prisoner, but I was alive. I had my life. I wondered how long I would be held captive. How long would the war last? Who would win? "Don't think too much! Just hold on!" I kept repeating in my mind. I knew I couldn't let myself get scared or angry. Especially not angry. People do unwise things when they're angry. I had to hold on.

I was told to get into the sidecar. I wrapped the blanket around my shoulders. We drove inland now and quickly arrived at a group of buildings. By that time I was stiff with cold and the warming effect of the liquor was long gone. I had noticed signs that told me we were in the vicinity of Cisterna. Now we were approaching higher ground and a group of houses. We stopped in front of a three-story building. I would be told later that this was the zone command for the German troops. My captors led me to the ground floor of the building where a large group of Allied prisoners were being held in a crowded room. I later learned that this whole building and the surrounding buildings housed Allied prisoners, most of them Rangers from the First and Third Batallions who were captured during the previous night's incursion against Cisterna. The Rangers had been created a couple of years earlier to mirror the daring British commandos. Already they were famous for their stealth and feats of courage.

I was brought before another officer for interrogation. This one spoke perfect English and told me he had attended college in the United States. After asking brief and routine questions, he gave me a pack of German cigarettes. Then I was taken to the third floor where some thirty Allied officers were being held. Once in the room, my captors led me to the fire where Ranger Captain Chuck Schuster was sitting. Schuster was the ranking Allied officer, which meant he was our commandant. My captors made a point of introducing me to Captain Schuster, because the German commander, I learned, had given orders that I was to be Captain Schuster's interpreter. The captain merely nodded when I acknowledged my assigned role.

The Ranger Captain

After the German soldiers left the room, I took off my boots. As I was pouring water out of them, the Ranger Captain, without looking at me, quietly asked how I was captured. I told him the details of my crash landing in the bay and my capture by the young German soldier on the beach. As I spoke, Captain Schuster continued to stare into the fire. He didn't nod and he never looked at me. But I assumed he was listening.

By picking up bits and pieces of conversation from other soldiers in the room, I learned the details of the crushing defeat suffered by the Rangers in Cisterna. There were many dead and wounded. From what I could piece together, Captain Schuster and his men had been cut off and trapped. The Captain had called and called for backup but there was none. The Rangers, under the desperate leadership of the Captain, had fought on alone as long as they could and much was lost.

I would later be told that it was Captain Schuster whom the famous Colonel Darby—leader of the legendary "Darby's Rangers"—had relied upon to carry out some of the Rangers' most dangerous and bloody missions. Captain Schuster was the perfect image of a daring Ranger. He was tall and powerfully built, a tribute to his years of weightlifting while he worked as, of all things, a cake decorator back in Boston. He was what girls in those days called "tall, dark and handsome," in a brooding, Tyrone Power sort of way. As American war heroes go, this Captain Schuster both looked and acted the part. I could see that his men held him in high regard, and he received their respect as a matter of course and with a decidedly cool detachment.

Just as I was passing out the cigarettes the interrogator had given me, the room fell silent as we focused on the familiar whine of planes approaching. Bombers. As the sound grew to a rumbling growl that was nearly overhead, we realized that our buildings were the likely target of Allied planes unaware of our presence here. They probably thought they were simply attacking a German command post! When we hit the floor, I couldn't help thinking what a bum deal it would be to survive all this and then get it from one of our own! But, I don't know, maybe it was because I was so tired, I saw the whole situation as kind of ridiculous—not even real. I didn't have a sense that we were going to be killed. It was all just irritating.

Bombs were screaming and exploding now all around us, very close. Machine-gun bullets tore the ceiling and wall to pieces. This was my first experience at this end of a bomb, and my teeth, my eyeballs, and my brains felt as if they were being shaken loose. My ears were ringing. I had no helmet, so I covered my head as best as I could with my arms. I remembered learning that you should keep your mouth open in an explosion, I guess so that your head doesn't blow up. So I opened my mouth, wide. One explosion was so close that our whole building shuddered and I felt it in my guts and the top of my head. (Maybe that open-mouth thing was really true.) Then there was silence. Oh, I could hear distant yelling and trucks starting up but compared to the bombing, it was silent...a deadly, strange silence. When we got up and looked out of the window we saw a horrible sight. A bomb had penetrated the roof of the building next door, exploding as it hit. I heard someone say that Allied prisoners, mostly Rangers, were being interviewed in that building.

Later no one spoke as we lay on the floor, trying to get

some rest. I don't know how long the shouting and truck sounds lasted. I knew they were carrying bodies of our guys out of the building. I could see it all in my head. I hated that vision. I was ashamed of finding the bombing merely irritating while our men were dying next door.

Finally I was able to blank out the images by reviewing all that had happened to me since I had arrived at Capodichino that morning. When I got to the part about my engine temperature overheating, I started to feel angry. What in the hell had happened? Everything had checked out before takeoff—I was always very careful about that. We had top-notch mechanics, and I was in the habit of taking care of them. I kept them well stocked with the best liquor rationed to us, to show, you know, my appreciation for their good work. After all, a pilot wants to be sure his mechanic will go the extra mile for him, and I believed mine did. I *knew* mine did. What could have gone wrong? When I thought about my plane, it didn't have an engine at all but was like a big black kite. I guess I was actually dreaming, because then everything started to unravel and I was flying above the houses where we were being held and I could see bombs exploding.

Next morning we were loaded onto trucks and taken to a large train station just south of Rome. No one said anything about the bombed-out building next door. The smell was terrible, but we all tried not to look at it as we passed by. No one said a word about it. Captain Schuster's face looked like a mask. He was silent and still. I stayed nearby in case I had to interpret for him. But even the Germans were quiet so he had no need of my services.

When we arrived at the train station, the officers were taken to a waiting room that was surrounded by large, dirty glass windows. The enlisted troops were sent to the car barns.

As I sat there in the train station, I couldn't help thinking, "I've been gone for almost a whole day. Do they think I'm dead, or do they realize I've been captured? What about my motorcycle? Did someone take it back to Naples? Will they be notifying my family? Don't think about that stuff! Think about escape. Find a way to escape! Fill your mind with ESCAPE. ESCAPE!"

We weren't in the train station very long when sirens signaled another Allied bombardment. I tried to get as far away from the massive floor-to-ceiling windows as possible! Fortunately it didn't last long and the building was spared. It seemed the Allies were after the tracks and not the station. Thank the Lord, there were no injuries.

The bombing had interrupted the Germans' transportation of prisoners, so I took advantage of the confusion to speak with one of the guard soldiers. I was trying to find out where we were going. Suddenly a German officer entered the station and began reprimanding the soldier for not standing at attention while speaking to me! Apparently the soldier was required to pay me the same courtesies he would pay any officer, enemy or not! Discipline is so important in a repressive regime that I suppose they have to condition people to respect authority no matter what.

Soon they were packing us onto trucks again. It was customary for officers to be loaded last and it happened that I was the very last to board the truck. Just before I stepped up, the young Nazi guard I had been talking to rushed over to me and, without even making eye contact, slipped me a loaf of bread he had hidden under his coat. If this boy had been caught, his punishment would have been severe.

Rome

My fluency in German probably saved my life. It likely helped in many ways from the moment of my capture. I tried to use it to help all the guys. What was clear to me from the start was who I was. Although my German upbringing made me at home in another language and Russian blood runs through my veins, I was and always will be an American first. That feeling seemed to expand the longer I was a prisoner. I would never have traded my "American-ness," not even for my precious freedom. Looking around at all the different guys from every part of the United States, whose ancestors had come from every part of the world, I would marvel at the wonder of it: we were all Americans. That's what made us strong then and what makes us strong still—all that blood mixed up—Irish, Polish, Greek, Norwegian...and that may be just one guy!

That's why we were and still are nearly unbeatable. As a people we're strong, smart, big (bigger than a lot of people in the world), and pretty tough and resilient in our attitude. Yeah, I think it comes down to attitude. I guess you could call it self-confidence, but it's mixed with compassion and humor for most of us. And that has taken us a long way. The Nazis tried to convince the German people that they were the superior race. They said it was because of their pure blood. But I think it's just the opposite. We had better stuff going into our war because we were these tough mutts—mixed bloods, if not biologically then culturally. Sure, there were plenty on our side who held onto their hate and fear of differences. But for many others the experience of war changed all of that, at least during combat. You may think you hate or fear someone who is different, but when you have to rely on him as your medic, your mechanic or your buddy, your attitude changes for the better and you get to see way beyond the superficial stuff, straight into what's really important and true.

When we got to Rome, the trucks pulled up and unloaded near the Coliseum. My earlier inquiries about where we were being taken had been met with silence, but this time I was told that all of the Allied soldiers would be paraded through the streets of Rome. We would begin at the Coliseum and march along the Imperial Forum, down Corso Vittorio something or other, the Via della I can't remember the name, all the way to the Via Aurelia (that name I can remember). The Germans hoped that this performance would demonstrate and exploit what they called the failure of the Allied landing at Anzio on January 22. Schuster sat stone-faced as I explained all of this to him. The darkness of his mood had not lifted since the previous night's bombing—not that I had yet seen much life in him since our first introduction. But he had survived a wretched battle and a failed mission and I understood his misery.

So there we were, the Allied Forces, a ragged lot of about seven hundred, dirty and tired, walking four and five abreast along the historic streets of Rome. Nearly every ten feet on either side of us marched an immaculate and erect German soldier, in perfect contrast to us, just right for the Nazi propaganda machine. We could see the German film crews riding ahead of us in open cars, recording all of this. Surely when that film would be shown in Germany, the voice on the newsreel would tell of the great Nazi victory over the Allies, and the German people would be bolstered by the news that we had suffered crushing defeats at the hands of their armies. They would be told that victory would soon be theirs. But what if the German people at home could have heard the quiet? What would they think then? For all of the numbers of Romans that the Germans were able to assemble to witness the march of Allied prisoners through their city, the crowds were oddly sedate, some even somber. Oh, there were a few cheers or a curse here and there with fists shaken at us but, considering the size of the crowd, this was no genuine hurrah. I see their faces in my mind even now. They appeared to be squinting against the sun. Some were shading their eyes with their hands. But there was something about their faces and their silence that told us there was no real joy in Rome that day. At least that's the way I remember it. And if I'm remembering correctly, the Romans had to know that their response, or lack of it, was dangerous.

I reasoned all of this much later. While it was happening I must have detached myself, because I don't remember feeling or thinking much of anything on that march through Rome, except for my great desire and firm commitment to escape. I felt certain that they planned to take us to Germany and I knew that I could not let them do that to me.

Prisons and Protocol

Following that shameful parade of propaganda, we were loaded onto trucks again and taken to an abandoned Italian prison camp a few miles outside of the city. As we lined up and approached our assigned barracks, my stomach lurched as I noticed that all prisoners were being body-searched. The line was moving too quickly! I couldn't think of what to do with the pocketknife I had in my pocket. In all the time since my capture, I had not been body-searched, and I had never given any thought to the damn thing. They'd see me if I just dropped the knife. I didn't want to do that. I had always had a pocketknife with me. It was a perfect tool and I had carried one since I was a kid. I wanted to keep it. I had to keep it.

Then I saw it—the latrine! Incredibly, the normally wary and suspicious Germans were pretty much in chaos. They were letting prisoners go to the latrine before being searched! Here was my chance. Off I went to the latrine, where I stashed my knife behind a door with the intention of recovering it later. I had been blessed again. I wonder how many other guys had slipped in there to get rid of stuff.

When I returned, the Germans were distributing a questionnaire which demanded our home addresses and family member names and their addresses. When I read it I knew that, as the only German-speaking prisoner, it would be up to me to get us out of answering those questions. But I also knew that I had to approach our captors carefully. It took me a few minutes to rehearse my statement, but then I made my stand, saying: "I feel that there must be some misunderstanding or error that has led us to be required to answer your questions. I have noted and do admire your strict adherence to protocol and therefore believe that your military would never wittingly violate any of the rules of the Geneva Convention, which states that prisoners give name, rank, and serial number only."

The other prisoners, not exactly sure of what I was saying, looked on in wide-eyed silence as the guards escorted me to the camp commander, where I repeated my cautious little speech.

Appearing before the camp commander did nothing to change my feelings. I wasn't aware of being afraid, exactly, just very mindful of my lowly position as a prisoner. So again I used my most respectful tone and chose my words carefully, appealing to the German sense of pride. I was very conscious of phrasing my request so that they could back down gracefully without losing face.

Responding with a definite coolness, the German commander finally, if reluctantly, agreed that the questionnaire was in error. Although his manner never approached friendliness, I detected a small bit of admiration for my grit.

In spite of their temporary lack of organization, the Nazis nevertheless treated rules and protocol like religion. That's what got us out of having to fill out that questionnaire.

Now I was told by my captors that I must have an orderly, even though I was the lone representative of the U. S. Air Corps, and Air Corps officers don't have orderlies. The Germans insisted that all officers have an orderly, and on this point Captain Schuster agreed. The Rangers had adopted the custom of orderlies and so he ordered me to go along. Well, I found a machine-gunner sergeant from a knocked-out B-25 bomber unit and asked him if he would be my orderly. He knew immediately that it would mean he would get better treatment and so he happily accepted.

Having heard that we were heading to the north, I asked the guard if it would be possible for my orderly and me to have warmer clothes. Immediately we were escorted to a kind of shed-like building where the floor was covered with Italian military uniforms. You could just imagine those Italian soldiers, sick to death of this bloody war, shedding their uniforms when Italy declared an armistice back in November and turning their backs on the military forever. The two of us, cold and dirty, were happy to choose two jackets and matching berets. "Not a bad deal," I thought, "this orderly business!" The clothes brought me more than just comfort, because I knew that now I could probably pass for an Italian. Shortly after that, an American officer lent me a long overcoat and the extra warmth helped a lot. There's a story about that officer and I'll get to that later.

I knew not to talk about escape with my fellow prisoners. You can't trust anyone in a camp. Some, I guess, were willing to trade what information they had. But more often you never knew who might be forced into a position where they had to tell what they knew in order to save their lives or someone else's. For now, I kept my own counsel and waited for everything to come together in its own time.

Meanwhile I learned a thing or two about hunger—real hunger. The food in camp wasn't fit for dogs. Some of the men suffered from diarrhea and dysentery. The only meal of the day consisted of a greasy lamb soup (at least we thought it was lamb) and some black bread. Some said the Germans put sawdust in the bread to give it texture. I couldn't bring myself to drink the dark, shiny broth, so I ate what there was of the meat

and the dry black bread for bulk and joined in the incessant conversations the men had about food.

"My ma makes the best meatloaf of anybody. She always
serves it with mashed potatoes, creamed corn, and homemade
biscuits or sometimes corn bread hot out of the oven."

"Aw, y'all haven't lived 'til you've eaten creole.
Godawmighty, them shrimps in creole sauce..."

"What is creole, anyway?"

"Hey, Mauritz, I hear you have some butchering experience. What's your favorite kind of steak?"

"You ever make sausage? My father makes sausage."

"Right now I'd sell my soul for some good hot chili and
a cold beer.... You ever heard of Cincinnati chili?"

Even Captain Schuster, our CO, the legendary Ranger,
would join in and talk about his days as an accomplished cake
decorator, describing for us the magnificent towering cakes he
adorned with flowers, garlands, doves, and columns made of
sweet, tinted, butter cream icing. *"Happy Birthday Dad,"*
"Good Luck Ann and Harry," "Welcome Home Charlie."

It would go on for hours, that talk of food, along with a
little baseball and a lot of not talking about women. You see, the
way it works is, when you're hungry, you talk about food. Only
when your belly's full do you talk about women; in between,
you talk about sports.

One other topic kept surfacing in camp: our fate. It was
pretty well known that we would likely end up being taken to
Germany. And we had all heard the stories about the camps in
Germany. But, as I've said, I was determined from the beginning not to let them take me. I just knew that I could not go
there. I can't tell you what it was or any more than that, but it
was as strong and clear a feeling as I have ever had. It was prob-

ably all that talk and the sight of the Germans in disarray that led me to confide in the CO about my determination to escape. "Captain Schuster," I began, "I have a plan to escape from here and I'm requesting your permission to do so."

As usual he showed no expression. Didn't even look up at me. So I continued, "I know it's my duty to try, and I feel very strongly that I must make my break before we are taken to Germany. I don't want to go there."

"Neither do I," Schuster said quietly and was silent for a moment. Then he said, "Me and the lieutenant here have been talking about the same thing. You seem pretty confident that you can pull this off. What makes you so sure you can do it?"

"Well, sir," I said, "the Germans are disorganized right now. I figure the fighting at Anzio is distracting them and I don't want to wait until they get things straightened out. I've got to go soon."

Now, for the first time, he looked at me. "I think the three of us might be able to work together. You understand?"

I can't say that I was surprised. I can't say that I was happy. (It was hard to be happy in a prison camp.) But I did have the feeling that I had helped him make up his mind. Oh, he and his lieutenant friend may have been talking about escape, but I don't think it was a solid thing with them as it was with me. I told him I just knew we'd be put in boxcars and sent to Germany, and I wasn't about to let them do that to me.

There was something about me that Schuster responded to, I know that now. Not that I was so special. But while he was very tough with his own men, he treated me with a kind of respect. I say "a kind of" because it was subtle. I do think he felt safer with me somehow. He saw and appreciated that I had good judgment and thought things through carefully. Rangers were trained to be dynamic and charge ahead. They had to go forward into great danger and sometimes do the impossible any way they could. I feel that he liked the way I sort of held back to study and evaluate. He knew I could hold myself together. It wasn't that he didn't trust his men. He had a reverence for the Rangers, but he also had to maintain a certain image with them. He was the CO, after all, and he had his reputation to consider. I was beginning to see how much he prized his daring image— and why not? Perhaps he felt that he didn't have to be so careful around me. I also think he admired the fact that I was hellbent on getting out of there on my own and would figure out a good way to do it, the best way to do it.

I thought of all of this long after the fact. At the time, it didn't occur to me; I just thought about getting the hell out of there and I believed we would be a good team. I admired his strength, both physical and mental. I knew he was smart; he had a lot of savvy on the ground. His had been the fiercest kind of training and his actual battle experience had been brutal. My instincts told me we would balance each other nicely.

The Escape Plan

Because I was Captain Schuster's interpreter, no one became suspicious if we were seen talking, so we were able to work out an escape plan without endangering ourselves. This was what we devised: We would arrange for Schuster, his lieutenant friend, and me to be in the latrine alone. The lieutenant would pretend he was ill in order to attract the attention of a guard. Once the guard approached, Schuster and I would overcome him. Schuster was well trained in that kind of attack and could manage it easily. I would dress in the guard's uniform and pretend to accompany the staggering lieutenant, with the help of Schuster, to the infirmary. On the way, we would escape.

But our plans were thwarted on February 8 when they suddenly loaded us onto trucks for a trip north to another prison camp.

Before we left, I did manage to slip into the latrine to retrieve my knife from behind the door. Once on the trucks, Captain Schuster and I were seated next to each other. It was then that we discussed cutting the canvas that was covering us, and throwing ourselves from the slow-moving truck convoy. But by nightfall the convoy speeded up considerably and we scrapped the idea as too dangerous. We could tell we were going up into a more mountainous area and the roads were getting rougher. Most of us slept off and on, but it was cold and uncomfortable. There wasn't much talking. We were all just trying to get through it.

It was about ten in the evening and very cold when we arrived at a new prison camp. It was in a town called Laterina.

The camp was a former Italian prison camp. It consisted of about twelve barracks. The cold was unbearable inside our barrack. There was no fireplace or stove, so we tore pieces of wood off the bunks and built a fire on the concrete floor. In the morning a German officer entered the barrack and, seeing remnants of the fire, reprimanded us for destroying government property.

In this new prison a Major Haggard of the Mechanized Calvary was now the highest-ranking officer, replacing Captain Schuster as commander of all of the captured troops in Laterina. Schuster and I were certain that from here we would likely be sent to Germany. As soon as we were settled in, Captain Schuster found an opportunity to inform Major Haggard of our decision to attempt an escape. The major gave Schuster his blessings for the two of us. The lieutenant was no longer included in our plan, as Schuster had decided three would be too risky.

Major Haggard was a West Pointer who had been brought to Laterina a little ahead of us. He had actually been with us for a short time back in the first prison camp outside of Rome. This major and his orderly had gotten lost behind the front at Anzio where the Germans captured the two of them, jeep and all! Haggard was the officer I mentioned earlier, who, back in that first camp, had given me his overcoat. He could spare a coat because he had had all of his belongings with him at the time he was captured. So when we approached him now, I gave his coat back to him.

"Thank you for the use of the coat, sir," I said, handing it over. I figured that if we made it out I couldn't be wearing an American officer's coat and if I didn't make it, well, I sure as hell wouldn't need a coat then.

Captain Schuster and I knew the major could have denied us permission to escape, because the Germans had said they would kill two enlisted men for every officer who attempted to break out! But without hesitation the major had given his approval, saying it was our duty to try. We were all of the same mind then, believing you had to go nose to nose with those Germans and dare them to make good on their threats…and, of course, pray to God that they wouldn't!

There were some, of course, who didn't agree with this. They felt that once they were captured, the war was over for them and they could just wait it out, not that it was comfortable, or even tolerable. A prison camp is not without its dangers, but I understood that some guys found a prison camp better than the shooting and killing, better than the horror of battle. I understood that. But that wasn't true for me and it wasn't true for Schuster. Somehow I thought it was worse to be a prisoner. Not that I loved battle the way Schuster seemed to. Schuster craved the fight. He was trained for it, he did it well, and as I was to learn later, he truly loved it. The killing, I mean.

While Schuster watched out for the guards, I slipped out of the window in our barrack into the empty barrack next to ours through a window that opened easily. My goal was to get a better look around the camp in all directions, without a guard watching me. Running from window to window, boosting myself up here and there so that I could see beyond the next building, I got a good idea of how things were laid out and was able to draw a decent-enough map of the camp. After darting back to our barrack, Captain Schuster and I devised a plan of escape. If it worked, we could pretty much walk away! *If* it worked. We were counting on a lot of things going our way, not the least of which was that all of the windows would be as rotted and easily opened as the ones we had tried so far.

While I was in the empty barrack, I found some India

ink and some shoe polish. We figured these things had been left by some former prisoners who had probably received them from the Red Cross or some other outfit. I brought this loot back to Schuster and explained that I could use the shoe polish to darken my hair so that I could look more like an Italian. With his dark eyes and thick black hair, Schuster would easily pass for a Latin.

"With the ink," I told Schuster, "we can blacken our boots. I've noticed that the Italians don't wear anything but black high-top shoes, and our brown military boots might give us away."

Quickly we darkened our boots with the ink and my hair with the shoe polish. When we were finished, we thought our boots could pass if no one looked too closely. My hair, on the other hand, made me look like the villain in a bad play, and I felt as if my head was caked with lard. But from a distance, we figured, my new look would pass muster. We hid the empty ink bottle and shoe-polish tin and positioned ourselves to make our move. If a guard saw us now, especially me with my darkened hair, it would be all over. We had to get out fast.

Fortunately the guards were only watching the occupied barracks. Schuster figured that if we timed it just right, we could both sneak from our barrack to the unoccupied one next door, where I had been before. Then we'd move on through the next two empty barracks until we got to the double fences that surrounded the camp. In all we had to get through three empty barracks inside the fences and one more outside.

We watched, and at a moment when none of the guards appeared to be looking in our direction, we crawled out of a window and darted to the barrack next to ours, getting in through the same window I had used before. It seemed fast and easy but we still had a way to go. Again we watched and waited and at last found the right moment to slip into the next empty barrack. Again this window opened easily. As soon as we were inside the second barrack (again crawling through a window) we looked out of the window at the other side, waited for the guard to disappear, and dashed to the next and last barrack, climbing in through the window, as easy as that. Now we saw our first real obstacle. There between the fences, two young Italian men were bent over, working with some electrical wire.

"What about those two?" I asked Schuster.

"I'll find out."

Opening the window slightly, the Captain said in a stage whisper, *"Signore! Signore! Tedeschi amicos—tedeschi cattivo?"* It was a crude way of asking, "Are you friendly with the Germans or do you think they are bad?"

The response came quickly. *"I tedeschi sono cattivi!* ("The Germans are bad!") whispered one of the Italians, turning his head only slightly to project his words in our direction while he remained in his bent-over position working with the wires.

Without changing his position and keeping his arm low at his side, the same Italian worker, who clearly understood what we were attempting, beckoned us to come. Now, the Italian signal for "come here" is different from our beckoning gesture. There would be times to come when that difference would confuse us, but in this instance we knew by his words and his manner that he meant to help.

From this barrack we could see a guard at the main gate. We could also see a guard to our right at the end of the barrack we were in, and we timed him as he supervised a prisoner work detail. He was walking back and forth, disappearing behind the barrack and coming out again at regular intervals. We managed to break off a piece of wood long enough to use as a makeshift crowbar. When the guard on our right disappeared from view and the guard at the gate was looking away from us, the Captain crawled out of the window, pried up the inside fence, darted past the Italian workers, and pried up the outer fence before heading for a final barrack outside the compound. On the way to that barrack was a ditch. As the Captain neared the ditch, the guard at the gate looked our way.

"Chuck, drop in the ditch!" I stage-whispered from my post at the window.

Down he went. The guard continued looking our way and my heart was pounding. "Please, don't let the guard see him!" Miraculously, the guard slowly turned away! God! I took a deep breath and again I signaled to him, "Now!" Schuster made a dash for the outer barrack and quickly disappeared inside through the window.

Meanwhile the two Italian workers, incredibly, continued as if nothing was happening. From the first moment when Chuck had called out to them they had, without hesitation, protected us with their cool deception.

It was my turn. When the two guards were in the right position, I crawled out of the window and under the inner fence. I stayed low to the ground as I made my way to the next fence. I felt no fear. I was only aware of trying to be quick and careful at the same time. As I came up beside the two Italian workers, they pretended to take no notice of me. Then I stole a glance at the guard at the gate and, to my horror, saw that he was looking in my direction! I remained hunched over, picked up some of the wire, and pretended to work alongside the Italians. I held my breath, wondering if now they might be so afraid of being caught aiding an escapee that they would turn me in. One word or ges-

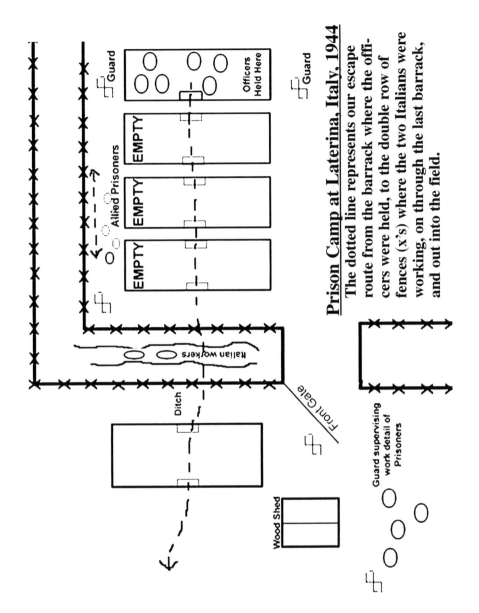

Prison Camp at Laterina, Italy, 1944

The dotted line represents our escape route from the barrack where the officers were held, to the double row of fences (x's) where the two Italians were working, on through the last barrack, and out into the field.

79

ture from them and I could be shot on the spot or hauled back to an even worse fate. My heart was beating so hard and loud that I almost missed hearing the whispered *"Aspetta! Aspetta!"*

I knew that word. "Wait!" They were telling me to wait! Now I knew that these good men would do nothing to give me away! They just kept on working, calmly, as if we had planned the whole thing. They knew what would happen to them if the Nazis caught them helping an escapee. Yet here they were, without a moment's hesitation, risking their lives to make it possible for me to blend in!

I kept my head down until one of the Italians called, *"Vai!"* (*"Go!"*) I dropped lower and scrambled under the outer fence and into the barrack where the Captain was waiting. There was no time for thanks or even a nod. But I pray to God that I never forget those two who saved me from being caught.

"Close call out there, Mauritz," the Captain said.

"You see what those workers did?"

But Schuster only motioned for me to join him at a window facing away from the compound. As we angled our bodies so as not to be seen from the outside, I saw the woodshed that I had sketched on my map. There a German guard had a detail of prisoners chopping wood. The shed itself might shield us as long as the guard didn't turn around. But before we could devise a plan, a piercing siren screamed. Schuster and I could only look at each other in horror as we flattened ourselves against the wall. We were caught! My mind raced, trying to think what to do. But there was nothing. Nowhere to run without being shot. In a second, the guards would storm this outer barrack and get us. But as minutes passed, nothing happened. Nothing. When we looked out of the window again, we saw that the guards at the wood-chopping detail were calmly lining up the prisoners two abreast and marching them slowly toward the main gate.

Could it be? Oh, Merciful God! It was chow call! We couldn't have timed our escape more perfectly. In truth, we hadn't timed it at all. The grace of God had guided us to the best place possible for escape at the moment the mid-day siren went off. And the grace of God, I now understand, also placed those two Italians in that unlikely spot between the two fences, saving us from being caught. It all came together for us and we walked out of that German prison camp into freedom. We walked out, simple as that.

On the Run

Stepping from our imprisonment on February 9, 1944, sometime around the noon hour, we found that freedom took the form of vast, wide-open fields, with no protective trees or bushes. We didn't dare run and could not have done so anyway. The fields were covered with a sticky, damp earth that clung to the soles of our shoes and quickly built up into huge clumps, forcing us to shake our feet every few steps. Our big American feet, made bigger by the damp Italian soil, were leaving a clear trail to follow. The sluggishness of our gait became the stuff of nightmares—you're being chased by something awful but can only run in slow motion. We did not look back. There were no sounds to indicate that we had yet been discovered or were being followed or chased. Still, every nerve was tensed and ready for the scream of a siren, distant gutteral shouts, the barking of dogs, or the tat-tat-tat of machine-gun fire.

But the only sounds were our own breathing and the soft, padded thumps of our feet sinking into the moist, black soil. When we had put about a hundred yards between us and the compound, our hearts stopped when a man appeared, like an apparition, in the field, walking calmly toward us. It wasn't clear to us what he was doing there, but he was obviously an Italian. He wore the clothing of a farmer and he approached us in a friendly and casual manner.

Because Schuster had been in Italy for a while and had picked up a good bit of Italian, he did the talking. *"Buon giorno, signore,"* he ventured, trying to sound calm.

"Buon giorno!" was the genial reply.

Once again, Schuster got right to the point in his broken Italian. *"Tedeschi, buono or cattivo?"* ("Do you think the Germans are good or bad?")

"I tedeschi sono cattivi!" was the man's resounding reply as he spit into the black soil.

"Buono," answered Schuster.

Now I joined in. *"Fumo?* Smoke, cigarette?" I tried, as I pantomimed smoking.

"Sigaretta? Ah, *si, si,"* he said, pulling out a pouch of loose tobacco and papers. He deftly rolled me a cigarette and, like a magician, handily produced a large, lit match.

"Grazi, signore," I said, greedily taking a few quick, deep drags as we started off again.

"Buona fortuna!" he called. ("Good luck!")

We walked off, still trying to appear casual and unhurried. But by now I was so dizzy from the strong tobacco that I had to make a great effort not to stagger. That stuff on a very empty stomach made my Luckys, and even the German brand I had been given, seem like nothing at all!

We went about another hundred yards, with me still woozy from the cigarette and both of us doing our strange little dance of walk two or three steps, shake our feet, and so on. Finally we reached the blessed protection of the woods. Once inside, we discovered a path that eventually became a country road. Soon we approached a tiny village where the houses were set back from the dirt road. To my right, an elderly woman came out of one of the houses and hurried toward us.

"What in the hell?" said Schuster. "Don't move or say anything."

From under a shawl the old lady pulled a small bundle wrapped in a clean cloth. She handed me the bundle and ran

83

off, disappearing into her house. At that moment even the ever-wary Captain Schuster didn't pause to consider the possibilities. As if we had been beguiled or stupefied by the old woman, we calmly and obediently looked inside. Well, our trust, or foolhardiness, was rewarded, because there inside we found sausages and bread!

Without a word to each other, we ate like ferocious dogs and continued down the road.

With some food in me and the comfort of a few miles between us and the compound, I was able to absorb the details of what had happened. The ease of our escape was amazing to me, but what was filling my thoughts were those Italians we had encountered: first, the two working inside the fences who had risked their lives by not turning us in; then the man in the field, just steps from the camp, who gave me a smoke; and finally the old lady who ran out of her house with food for us.

"I can't believe this," I said to Schuster, "these Italians..."

"Don't get too confident," he cut in. "There are plenty of *Fascisti* who will be happy to turn you in or kill you—*molto* happy. And what these *Eye*-talians are telling me is that we're awfully damn obvious looking. We got to get some better clothes."

The Captain was right. And now that we were approaching a more populated area, we decided to take a chance and try to get some clothes that would help us blend in better than these old Italian military uniforms did. I knew that Schuster would be willing to steal clothes—or even kill for them, if he had to.

Once in the village, Schuster selected a house and knocked on the door. Using his broken Italian and lots of gestures, the Captain asked if we might come in, taking a chance by admitting to the elderly man who opened the door that we were Americans—*"americani, scapati de Laterina"* (*"escapees from Laterina"*). And he told him we needed help.

"Si, endrate," he said quietly, motioning for us to slip inside after checking to make sure no one was watching. After bolting the door, the man, an older woman (his wife, I assumed), and a younger woman with a baby (probably their daughter and grandchild) stared at us as Schuster continued our story of escape from the prison camp. Smiling and using a charm I hadn't seen before, the Captain explained our need for clothes, showing the family that we were still wearing our American uniforms (I was in my flight suit) under the things we had been given back in the camp. Any clothes we got we would put on over our uniforms. It was important that we keep our uniforms on so that we would not be taken for spies.

While Schuster was speaking, I could not tell what the family was thinking. They just stood there quietly, listening solemnly and nodding occasionally. At last, the old man's face softened and he said, *"Ah, si, volete dei vestiti"* ("Yes, you need clothing"). In rapid-fire Italian he issued orders to his family. No sooner said than done!

I stood in wonder as the women produced old pants, shirts, and heavy jackets. Here in this tiny house, which was not more than two small rooms built around a large fireplace, this humble family was, like the others, willing to risk terrible consequences to give us the clothes we needed. And oddly enough, they seemed to have produced them out of thin air.

"Here, take this, please," I said, handing the man my broken watch in a pathetic attempt to repay him. Our host did me the honor of graciously accepting my offer. But this grand old gentleman who stood straight as a fence post could not be outdone. In return for my gift, grinning a nearly toothless grin, he gave me a cap. What a treasure that would be! If I pulled it down low, I could hide my hazel eyes.

We did give the family our chits and explained that they could be presented to our troops when they came through—if they made it this far north—for reimbursement in cash. But in giving the old man my watch I wanted to give him something personal, something to express my gratitude. I think he understood.

The pale February sun was beginning to angle into late-afternoon shafts when we left after a quick dinner of goat cheese, some black olives that had been fried in olive oil, a piece of crusty bread, and a couple of glasses of red wine. They wished us well and made us understand that they would pray for us, gesturing toward the lit candle they had in front of a small holy statue in the corner.

Night would soon close in on our first day of freedom. I hadn't thought of the men back at the prison camp at all. When I did, I tried to tell myself that nothing had happened to them on our account. As for Capodichino, well, that now seemed worlds away. Captain Schuster kept wondering how far we were from the American lines. We didn't know where the lines were now. Had the Allies succeeded at Anzio? We were in the dark. We knew it had to be a great distance to the front, but we didn't even know if we were walking in the right direction. At the very least, we hoped we were putting miles between ourselves and the prison camp. But we weren't even certain of that! We were in hilly terrain; without a compass or a map, we knew it could be tough.

"If the front is too far away, we could head for the Mediterranean and try to meet up with a destroyer," Schuster suggested.

"The Mediterranean is that way, west," I replied, pointing left, "and, I'm guessing, not too far as the crow flies. But wouldn't there be a lot of activity there and a good chance—"

"Yep, we could be recaptured. Dense population that way, thick with Nazis, *Fascisti* too. Too bad we aren't crows, huh, Mauritz...or had one of those slick little fighter planes of yours so you could get us out of this."

"What about north?" I said, ignoring the sarcasm. "Through the mountains, the Italian Alps, then up into Switzerland or maybe France. I wish we had a map and a compass."

"Sounds safer. We could stay away from cities. But, you know, the cold in the mountains. I mean, it might be pretty desolate with long stretches between civilization. And I think it would be just too far to the border."

"Yeah, that's no good. I mean, we could die in those mountains trying to get through. At this time of year," I said, "it won't work."

"East is what we got," Schuster finally concluded. "I wonder how far the Adriatic is from here."

"It's hard to guess without knowing exactly where 'here' is. We know we're not all that far from the Mediterranean, but there are some big mountains between us and the Adriatic."

Ancona! Ancona!

Now the road was climbing. Soon we were on a hilltop where a man came out of a house as if to meet us. Schuster extended a hand. *"Buonasera,"* he ventured.

"Buonasera!" the man answered warmly.

Again Schuster, flashing his best movie-star smile, took a chance and explained in his broken Italian, *"'mericani...pris-*oners...*scapate.* Escape today. We need to find our com-rades...*soldati 'mericani...capire?"* With a word here and there and gestures, he made it clear that we needed to know how far we were from the American lines and in what direction we should be walking.

The man pointed out that we should be heading east toward Ancona and the Adriatic where he had heard that British subs were picking up escaped prisoners. But, he added, we would need to cross the Arno River in order to get started in that direction. Not a big river, but a river nonetheless, he explained with a broad smile.

"Bridges will be guarded," Schuster said, turning to me. But we had no reason to worry, because our friend, who seemed to be enjoying himself, happily and proudly announced that he just happened to be the proprietor of a *traghetto*, a ferry, that crossed the very river in question.

In no time we were climbing into a tiny, battered dinghy (hardly the "ferry" we had envisioned). Its owner, short and bar-rel-chested with a perpetual smile, told us, as though he, per-sonally, had somehow arranged it, that the Arno flowed all the way to Pisa. But again he emphasized with happy authority, while pointing toward the darkening sky, that we shouldn't think about going anywhere but Ancona.

"Quanto e lontano Ancona?" Schuster attempted.

("How far to Ancona?")

"About 140 kilometers," our friend replied, turning down the corners of his mouth and making the tilting Italian hand gesture that means "more or less."

"*Sopra montagna?*" ("Over the mountains?") Schuster asked.

"*Si, si,*" said the man.

"Well, we got a mountain range in front of us, Mike, before we see the lights of Ancona and those British subs."

"Ancona! Ancona!" the boatman sang in a surprisingly high tenor voice as he pulled on the rope that hauled us across the little river, and he rhymed "Ancona" with a phrase in Italian I neither understood nor remember. We would come to hear many such Italian rhyming songs, some light and witty and some rich with bawdy humor, sarcasm, and a disdain for pomposity and self-importance, especially when it came packaged in the form of government rules and rulers. It was odd to think that Italians, who are so masterful at turning a serious aversion into hilarious and biting ridicule, could have allied themselves with the rigid, rule-loving Nazis. If I learned nothing else from this experience, I would carry with me for life the lesson that a war is fraught with contradiction. Very little is what it at first appears to be. We were warmed by our boatman's cheerful song and his assurances. We said our goodbyes and thank-yous with renewed spirit and purpose.

Another small miracle had unfolded, and as the sky leaned toward darkness, we headed in the direction of Ancona and, we hoped, the British subs. As we climbed up the bank from the river, I saw that we had another, steeper climb out of the river valley in order to head due east. Schuster was quite a distance ahead of me, taking the hill like a bulldozer. But my feet and ankles, unaccustomed to long treks in hilly terrain, were now aching, swollen, and cramping.

"Let's go, Mauritz!" called the Captain from near the top of the hill. "I know those big, precious fly-boy dogs of yours are probably killing you, but you better move or spend the rest of the war down in that valley."

When I finally got to the top, Schuster was sitting with his back to me. I hadn't even caught my breath when he pointed to a light coming from a farmhouse. I knew it meant taking a chance again. I prayed this would be a family of partisans—*"Patrioti."*

We walked up the narrow path. Schuster took a breath and knocked on the old, unpainted farmhouse door. The door creaked open about six inches to reveal the weathered face of a farmer.

"Si?" he inquired warily.

Again Schuster explained, *"Soldati 'mericani, signore. Scapati tedeschi a Laterina. Sonno...*ah, I mean, sleep. We need a place to sleep tonight, *sta notte,"* he said, tilting his head on his hands and closing his eyes.

"Ahhh, per dormire sta notte. Si, si," was the farmer's response. Then he told the captain, "I don't like the Germans. I don't want them here. But my family and I have to be careful. Laterina isn't so far away, you know." Then pointing, he added, "You can sleep in the shed over there. I'm sorry, I wish I could do more, but I can't. You'll be safe there and you can get some rest."

"Grazi, buonasera," Schuster said, "I mean, *buonanotte."*

The door closed.

We headed for the shed, just steps from the house, next to a small granary. Inside the shed it smelled of damp earth and old wood. The little shack offered no relief from the cold, but as our eyes adjusted to the darkness, we saw something piled to one side and covered with burlap sacks. Walnuts! Not the ideal bed but far better than bare earth. By the time we had removed our boots and covered ourselves with the burlap sacks, the place felt like the Ritz.

But before we could close our eyes, there was a light

tapping at the shed door. As it creaked open, I prepared myself to see Nazi or *Fascisti* soldiers. To my great relief it was the old man.

He handed Chuck a jug of water and something tied up in a clean white cloth.

"*Grazi tante,*" said the Captain.

"It isn't much, I'm sorry," he said to Chuck in Italian, "but it will fill your bellies, I think." Then he went back toward the house, carrying a small lantern.

We each took long drinks of water from the jug and decided that we'd wait until morning to eat. We were tired to the depths of our souls that night and for many nights to come. Even though the shed was the crudest of shelters, there was something profoundly restful about coming in from the out-doors. It wasn't just our relief from the fear of being spotted and recaptured. Humans can only be out under the open sky for so long before extreme physical, mental, and spiritual exhaustion overtakes them. Having a roof over your head brings great com-fort and a sleep that is so yielding and so deep that it's more like losing consciousness. Still, I will never forget that in my last remaining seconds of wakefulness I was tormented by the ghost of that threat made by the Germans back at the prison camp. Images of Nazi prison guards filled my head. I saw them dis-covering us missing and making good on their promise to shoot two enlisted men for every officer who escaped. Did they carry out their threat? "Please, dear Lord," I silently begged, even though He hadn't often heard from me, "don't let it be so."

Free Birds

I know I didn't dream during that first night of freedom, lying on that mattress of walnuts under burlap sacks. I slept as still and soundly as a dead man. When I finally opened my eyes, I saw gray light coming through a million cracks in the weathered wood. Schuster was already lacing up his boots. I was stiff with cold and my swollen feet felt as heavy as two logs. I ached all over and was reminded of an old, arthritic fellow who used to come into the butcher shop back in Turtle Creek. Whenever my boss asked how he was feeling, he'd answer, "I don't know what hurts best today."

When Schuster opened the bundle in white cloth, he found a generous hunk of cheese, a few thin slices of salami, and two large crusts of bread. We feasted on that breakfast and I almost forgot my aching feet until I stood to leave. Walking was going to be agony for me, but I had to get on with it. So off we went, heading toward the growing pink on the horizon.

Now as the sun rose, giving color to the landscape, I was struck by the beauty of this place. We were in steep hill country. In spite of the angry pain in my feet and ankles and the intense cold of the morning air, I noticed that even in February, this was a beautiful country. Much of the landscape was still green, even though it was winter. Exotic evergreens decorated the tumbling terrain. I later learned that they were mostly cypress. Every possible acre that could be put to use was cultivated. There were well-tended fields, vineyards, and orchards asleep under the benign winter sun, revealing themselves in every direction and angle of steepness, in shades of gold, tan, and mustard. You could see crumbling stone walls here and there, some along the roadway, some terracing off fields that rose like giant steps leading to heaven itself. All of the hills and valleys were dotted with little stucco or old stone farmhouses, some backing up right against the steep hillside so that there could be no doors or windows on one side of the house. Occasionally we would get a glimpse of a church or something more like a castle made of stone so old that it sometimes seemed to be part of the hillside, as if the whole structure was returning to the earth or had at least made a good marriage with it.

While I was enjoying all of this, I was reminded of the phrase "ancient footsteps," perhaps from a poem I learned in high school. On that first morning of our freedom when we felt like birds out of a cage, those two words just kept going around in my head. I kept thinking about how my miserable, aching feet were walking in these "ancient footsteps."

We stayed away from anything that resembled a main road, walking instead on paths and little country lanes. We kept checking the sun to make sure we were staying on an easterly course. The morning was so peaceful and beautiful that it was hard to remember there was a war going on. But I could always count on Schuster to bring me back to reality.

"We have to be careful in these hills. Someone could be watching us and we'd never know it. Never see 'em until it was too late. As we get closer to Ancona, there will probably be less country and more villages, more people and traffic on the roads, even the back roads."

"What we need is a map," I suggested.

"What I need is to get back," Schuster shot back. It was then that he talked for the first time about some of his war experiences—the raids and the killing, the intense training he had received to become a Ranger. He said his specialty was piano wire.

"You've killed people with piano wire?"

"It's the best way to do it. And I know lots of ways and I'm good at all of 'em. But piano wire is the best," the Captain said with a warm smile, as though he had just revealed his favorite method of tuning an engine. "We would wind it around the buttons of our uniforms—no one would ever know it was there."

This was the most animated I had seen Schuster. I could tell that he loved talking about this. Of course, I understood how necessary it was that we have men like him who can fight a war on such a personal level and take care of the business that can only be handled in that way. They do the work most of us would never do, and in the process they save countless lives with their courage and daring.

As for me, I had never wanted to carry a gun. My not having a weapon kept me from being killed when I was captured. Both Schuster and I knew that if we were recaptured, our chances of survival would be much greater if we were unarmed.

I always hoped, naively, I know, that my bombing and strafing had devastated property, stopping enemy production, troop and supply movement, destroying stockpiles, creating a diversion. I had no desire to kill human beings, even our enemies. If I did kill any, God help me. The intent to kill was never in me. But I admit that I would have done anything to protect and assist our troops on the ground. It's hard to be facing such terrible choices with the limited life experience many of us had brought to this war. But Schuster, he was young and yet very clear about what he was doing. Here I was listening to this war hero telling me not only that he could kill but that he would and did do so with relish—or at least that's what he thought or wanted me to think.

"Are you telling me that it doesn't bother you to kill a man?"

"Mauritz," he said, looking at me intently with his eyes narrowed, "I look at it this way: I'm not killing men, I'm just killing uniforms."

Who was I to judge this man? Schuster's contributions had saved American lives. I couldn't sort it out. This is good. That is bad. Where do I fit in in all of this? I had to look at the larger picture. Them against us. We're here to fight, and everyone has his own job to do. We're also here to win, and everyone has his own way to make that happen.

Loaves, Fishes, and Olive Oil

The next few days passed uneventfully. How could I have called them uneventful? Once you have known hunger, there is nothing uneventful about eating! It's a gift from God, a celebration, a miracle! We never went hungry now. The most amazing blessing of all was that very often we didn't even have to ask for food or drink. All we had to do was explain that we were American soldiers—*"soldati 'mericani scapate"*—from the Nazi prison camp at Laterina and we were offered a glass of wine, or a hot cup of the bitter, burnt barley they made into a substitute for coffee. As for food, these Italians shared it with pleasure.

I especially loved the delicious home-made cheeses, the fresh, crusty bread, the shiny black olives seasoned and fried in olive oil, the sausages, the tender, roasted rabbit, the chicken sautéed in wine and olive oil, the taste of rosemary and basil, the warm bean and pasta soups. It was hearty, life-sustaining peasant food, and these good people gave us whatever they had, which brought us much more than mere physical sustenance.

After a day of walking and climbing in the cold, I looked forward to taking off my boots and stretching out in a warm Italian kitchen. I grew to love hearing the crackle of garlic being sautéed in olive oil in a big black pan over the fire. The sputters and pops accompanied aromas that I came to associate with human comfort—smooth and zesty with a pure, earthy pungency that is Italy itself. A symphony of new, more energetic sizzles would assault you as delicate pieces of chicken, rabbit, venison, or even bread dipped in beaten egg and grated goat cheese would be sacrificed to the hot, seasoned oil in the giant iron pan. How those good cooks would smile at our salivating ooh's and aah's.

I hope I will always remember that there is nothing uneventful about eating, certainly not in Italy, where it has almost always been an event of grand and glorious proportions, made all the grander by the fact that in wartime and winter, these people were working with very little. I liken it to the Bible story of the loaves and fishes: it's what's in your heart, the desire to share and give, that brings about miracles of abundance.

Bathing, of course, was out of the question, though we washed up and even shaved occasionally, using pans of warm water and borrowed straight-razors. Shaving had more urgency for Chuck than for me with my unenthusiastic little showing of beard. But we both appreciated any opportunity to scrub off the sweat, dirt, and smell of our ordeal. Haircuts, which didn't require the trouble of warm water, were easier to manage. So all in all, our appearance was passable.

Sometimes we were offered money. It was usually the equivalent of only a few cents, but those lira would accumulate and eventually we would have enough to slip into a tavern for a sandwich and a beer. One afternoon we went into a little *barra* ("pub") that served hefty sandwiches of hot and sweet sausage with roasted red and green peppers. Because it was dangerous for us to speak in public, we were happy to just sit there stuffing our mouths and bellies when two German officers walked in.

"Boots!" I whispered to Chuck through my fat sandwich. By this time the black shoe polish we had used to camouflage our brown military boots had worn off. With every other Italian wearing nothing but black, I knew our boots could give us away.

We pulled our feet under the table and turned our ankles outward, forcing the soles of our shoes together in an effort to hide as much of the brown as possible. It wasn't the most comfortable position, but when you're eating Italian sausage and peppers on Tuscani bread, you could pretty much be hanging from the ceiling and still be content. Happily, the Germans didn't look at our feet; in fact, they didn't look at us at all. It could have been that they, too, were far more interested in downing one of those sausage sandwiches and a good glass of beer than in catching two dirty, ragged escapees.

————

One of the strange things about war is that when you made it through a close call, you usually didn't know why you were spared. Maybe your charade was actually working. Sometimes it was purely the gift of kindness or courage offered by strangers. Such people were everywhere, on both sides, in this war. They didn't see you as a threat and had no wish to bring harm to you just because you might be on the "other side." It's true. These things happen in a war. Sometimes the people who saved or protected you did it for political reasons. And sometimes the people who didn't turn you in or kill you looked the other way because it was easier and safer for them. They couldn't have known whether we were armed. I'm not saying they were cowards; maybe they just lost their nerve. Some were worn out from the war, tired and unable or unwilling to go along with it anymore. Others just knew how to play the odds, to pace things and evaluate the situation based on what would be best for them. Those German officers who walked into the pub might have been merely hungry and tired and more interested in a good meal and a few beers than in recapturing the two of us. Perhaps at that moment they preferred pleasure over business. That was unlikely, but you just never knew. That's what gets you finally. First you're afraid you're going to get caught or be forced to run or fight. Then when nothing happens, you usually don't know why. Looking back on it now, I guess the one thing that has really taken hold of me is that we are all just poor human creatures.

————

Although we were sometimes offered beds during those winter months, we came to love the barns that housed the farm animals. Italian barns were cozy and warm from animal heat, so warm that they were usually placed under kitchens in order to insulate the farmhouses. When we did sleep in beds, the *biancheria* ("bed linens") made by the farm women from flax, while immaculate, were rough and frigid.

Before going off to bed, we'd be given a long-handled, lidded pan filled with hot coals. We'd pass this bedwarmer over the sheets and jump in quickly. But on very cold nights the warmed *biancheria* would cool before our body heat could take over.

In winter the Italians often kept the kitchen door open. When I expressed surprise, I was told that they did this to keep the house from getting too smoky from the kitchen fire, which burned constantly. One farmer told us we would probably be just as surprised to learn that they kept their door closed in summer.

"Oh," I said, "to keep the kitchen cool?"

"No," he answered, "to keep the chickens out."

I loved studying the massive Italian fireplaces, which breathed so much life into the little stucco houses. The hearths were large enough for a man to stand in. You could poke your head in and look up and behold the wonder of succulent prosciuttos curing overhead. A cable with an ample hook held the family cooking pots. Sometimes there were little side-ovens where the baking took place, though I have heard that housewives in some Italian villages would mix and raise their bread dough and take it to a community oven for baking. One Italian I met who grew up in a little town in the Abruzzi region told me that the town baker would stand at the door of his establishment and call out the name of the family whose bread was ready. The village, he said, was so small that the families could hear him calling from their houses, or children playing outside and hearing the announcement would happily pass the word on to the appropriate family.

It was an effort not to think about my aching feet and legs. As a Ranger with lots of field experience, Chuck was in great shape for long-distance walking. I didn't dare complain to him, though. It's not that he didn't have a certain respect for fighter pilots, but sometimes he made remarks about our not really being down there in the thick of things. I was beginning to understand that Chuck's nature tended toward negativity and sarcasm, so I tried to steer clear of conversations that could lead to trouble.

As time passed, I began to get used to the constant walking and I could tell that my legs and feet were getting stronger. The terrain was rugged and even when we were walking through a valley, I knew that there was always a climb ahead.

We were obsessed with watching the sun (*"O Sole Mio"*) to be certain that we were always heading east and not veering off-course. But without a map, we were in fear of losing our bearings. It's not that easy to go straight in one direction when you're on foot in rugged terrain. Hell, experienced flyers get themselves lost flying over tabletop terrain like the desert.

Although we were also worried about being caught, we had no choice but to trust the Italians to point the way east to Ancona, the Adriatic Sea, and the promise of British rescue subs. We took our chances, hoping to avoid the Germans, the *Fascisti,* or even their sympathizers. We knew that Italy was in turmoil and its people torn apart. But we had to depend on the Italians and we simply had to bet on trusting the right ones.

We met a physician who was allied with the Italian partisans or underground. He told us that he couldn't visit his mother, because she lived with his *Fascista* brother. "I'd be a dead man if I did," he told us," but not before they tortured me to get me to talk."

"These Italians," I asked Schuster one day, "do you think we've been lucky, or are most of them in this part of the country on the side of the partisans? Were you briefed about this before Anzio?"

"Intelligence said it could be mixed. You know, it's like a civil war here. The hard-core Fascists—and there are plenty of 'em here—are more concentrated in the north. The *Patrioti* are in great danger from their own, and the Nazis, well, they're everywhere."

"We were told that the *Fascisti* and Nazis are telling the people that the *Patrioti* are Communists."

"Yeah, that's true," Schuster agreed. "*Communista*, they say. They all hate 'em. But only some of them are true Communists. Some are Socialists, some believe in democracy, and some don't give a damn—they just want the *Fascisti* and the Nazis crushed. And you know there are always people who play both sides. It's complicated and dangerous, and we can't trust anyone."

"I know," I conceded, "but I'm amazed at the good luck we've had so far."

"They said we could expect help from them, but you know what happens if they get caught. We've had reports of terrible torture everywhere. Fascists, Nazis, they all have it in for the *Patrioti*. That doctor who told us that he worried about his *Fascista* brother having him tortured wasn't exaggerating."

We could never be completely sure of our safety when we knocked on a door or approached someone. And I didn't like thinking that we could be endangering the lives of the people who were helping us. After all, some of these people weren't even helping us out of political conviction. Most of them were just simple farmers whose sons or brothers may have been off fighting somewhere. Hell, they probably just hoped that if their relative got in this same kind of jam, someone on our side, or the other, would do for him the way they were doing for us. I saw how religious they were. Every home had a little altar with statues of Christ or his mother. How these Italians loved Mary—*La Madonna*, they called her. I couldn't help but believe that some of this kindness was the fruit of their deep and abiding faith. But we knew that, no matter what their reasons for helping us, these Italians, if caught with us in their homes, would face terrible consequences.

Della Montagna

We were now leaving hill country and entering the more mountainous region of Tuscany. We had been mainly in valleys where there was no snow, but now we could see it on the hills and on the distant mountains. Those mountains with their peaks shimmering in the sunlight seemed far away from the war and the miserable little problems of mankind. When we looked at those rugged giants, I felt that we were looking at heaven where there was eternal peace. We may have mountains in Pennsylvania, but they're just big hills compared to the Apennines.

I was struck by something else, too: this was an ancient land. Lining the sides of roads everywhere were old stone walls that looked like part of the earth. In fact, they looked old enough to have been there since the Roman Empire. (I have since learned that they were, and some even before that!) Off in the distance you could see walled cities perched on hilltops. Some of the houses and churches were so old you could only stand there in awe. Most buildings in the States even one tenth that old would simply collapse. These people knew how to build. I remember a story I once heard about an American boy who went to study at Oxford. One day he was late for his class, so he ran into the classroom, slamming the door behind him. The instructor looked up and glared at him, saying, "Please go back and close that door properly, sir. That door, you see, is older than your country!"

But it was more than the buildings that appeared to have been there forever; it was the entire landscape, the trees, the fields, the vineyards, the roads and paths—many feet leaving those ancient footprints, many lives, many seasons. All of that had been in existence much longer than the fields and woods I knew back home around Turtle Creek.

This ancient mountain region had remained separate from the war and, I think, every war. Maybe that was it. From a distance it had seen many wars, ancient wars. Blood spilled down through the ages. Life, too. It was said that if a person living in Tuscany in the fourth century came back from the dead, he would find his house still standing and occupied.

These were all things I mulled over as we walked, but things I couldn't talk to Chuck about. First of all, Chuck was not much of a talker. But it was more than that. He wasn't interested in his surroundings. For instance, if I said, "Chuck, look at those mountains!", he might respond "Yep" on a good day. But most of the time that kind of comment from me would be met with silence or a little snicker—as if I was a little off or something. Chuck was intent upon his mission: to get back behind the lines, to get back into the war. It was as if Chuck thought that taking notice of things would somehow slow us down or make us soft.

From time to time, one thing did divert Chuck's attention: his appearance. He would claim that as a Captain and a Ranger he was duty-bound to maintain a certain image. He was proud of his physique, which had retained the tone and muscle of his body-building days in Boston. Given all of the walking we did, he sure didn't have to worry about his waistline. But when he got it in his head that he needed to have a shave, he didn't care how much trouble other people had to go through for him, he was going to have that shave. With his heavy black beard, Chuck's wanting a shave was understandable. But in these mountain villages, water had to be carried and heated in the fire, and it was the women who did the hauling. Yet Chuck never hesitated to ask, no matter what the hardship, and no one ever refused him. When he wanted something, the Captain could lavish as much warmth and charm as the best of them.

So while I was involved in, say, inspecting the finer details of a fourteenth-century house, Chuck could suspend his desire to get back to the war by losing himself in the essentials of good grooming.

———

One day, after walking for about ten hours, we came to a farmhouse. We decided to stop and inquire about the best way to get to Ancona. A smiling man of about thirty answered the door and when Captain Schuster told him of our situation, he welcomed us into his warm little kitchen with enthusiasm.

As soon as we were seated around the table, he produced a bottle of a light-colored liquor and three glasses. *"Salute!"* he toasted.

"Salute!" we returned, and enjoyed the warmth of the liquorice-flavored liquor. After a few more toasts, our host told us that the beans he had been cooking were about ready and he invited us to join him for his evening meal.

While we ate the tasty white beans with crusty bread, the Captain questioned our host further about the best route to Ancona.

"Over the mountains. *Montagna,"* he said. "No other way. And, you know, there will be snow there."

While Schuster and the man discussed our route to Ancona, I walked over to the fire and noticed a little shelf in a corner that contained a few old books. They looked like school books. As I leafed through one, I found a page with what appeared to be an out-dated but well-detailed map of Italy. *"Signore,"* I asked, holding up the book, "please, this could be a great help to us...this, this...aah, what's the word for map?"

"Carta," assisted Chuck. Using more Italian words than I knew, he asked if we could tear the map from the book and take it with us.

"Certainly," our host replied. "Who uses those old books anyway. Not me!" he added, laughing.

That map was a find. As a flyer I had to have knowledge of Italy, and I've always had a good sense of direction and an interest in geography. But being in the mountains without a compass was disorienting. I would often think of the young German soldier who took my survival kit when I was captured. He had just wanted money, so I probably should have bargained for the compass. But I had nothing to bargain. When he took that kit, he took it all.

We spent the night sleeping on the floor in front of the fire. Before dawn we were awakened by our host, who was dressed in a manner I had never seen before. He wore high boots that were laced up to the bottom of a pair of bright green knickers, and an equally colorful, heavy, knitted sweater covered by a sheepskin vest. To complete the outfit he wore a dashing hat with a feather in it so large that it brushed his shoulder and bobbed crazily when he walked and talked.

"Come, hurry! I'm taking you up into the mountains. I'll show you the way," he said with a theatrical sweep of his hand. "You see," he explained, spreading his arms wide so that we could take in his get-up, "today I am a mountaineer...*alpinista.*"

He apologized for not being able to provide us with mountain clothing like his, but we assured him we would be fine.   All vanity aside, we truly weren't in bad shape. We were wearing our combat boots and we had on our government-issue long johns, our uniforms and, on top of those, the clothing we were given at that first house near the prison camp. Along the way we had picked up knitted vests and some ragged scarves, gloves, and some old, worn caps.   But even if the weather had been warm, we would have kept our uniforms on. We would never have risked being be shot as spies if recaptured. Even though we had been blessed with great good luck, we still had to be careful everywhere we turned. As Schuster was fond of saying, we had to protect our asses. I heartily agreed.

After a quick breakfast of bread and what passed for coffee, we began the climb. It wasn't long before we entered the snow, but it was only a foot or two deep and temperatures were rather mild. Occasionally we encountered drifts that were deeper, but they were easy to avoid. Our climb was uncomplicated and we were able to enjoy the beauty of trees painted a glittering white, standing against the blue sky, arching under the weight of the snow. Some created a dazzling canopy over our heads. In the distance and all around us, more snow-covered mountains stood guard, high above deep valleys. The silence and peace of it all caused us to speak in hushed tones. How amazing that a terrible, bloody war could bring you to this paradise!

Before leaving us, our guide and host did his best to lay out a course that would bring us to a tiny mountain village by nightfall and on toward the Adriatic coast and Ancona. We thanked him and gave him our chits, hoping that once our guys reached him, he would be reimbursed for his kindness. He said he neither wanted nor expected any reimbursement from us. He told us that it had been his pleasure to help us. And so we all wished each other well. He told us to go first so that he could see that we were heading in the right direction. We turned to wave to him several times, chuckling as the great plume on his hat danced against the horizon each time he waved back at us, until we rounded a bend and walked out of his life forever.

Our good fortune continued as we made our way through the Apennines from village to village. One day after walking many exhausting hours through deep, crusted snow we decided to stop for the night. We struggled up to a small farmhouse and knocked at the door.

"Soldati 'mericani. Scapati. Molto fame," we called, and were graciously invited in. Once inside, we noticed a little girl of about ten whose face was swollen and purple. We inquired about her and were told that she was suffering from an infected tooth. We knew there was no possibility of a doctor or dentist treating the child. Her mother explained that she had given the girl cloves to chew in order to deaden the pain and that she would give her some wine and water to help her sleep. But that was the extent of the child's treatment unless her father were to decide to pull the tooth.

I wish I could write that we were able to help her. But we could do nothing except pat her hand and show our sympathy for her pain. When we left the next morning, the poor child was asleep with a white cloth tied up over her head, as our own mothers did when we had mumps.

Once we had said our thank-yous and left our chits behind, Schuster and I set off again in the snow. I thought about the differences between life in Italy and ours back in the States. Although life could be rough here, in many ways they had it good. They had a deep sense of family unity. Everyone had a large extended family close at hand. They had lived in their houses for generations, cooked in the same fireplaces that their great-grandmothers had cooked in before them, slept in the same beds they had been born in. In one tiny mountain hamlet we met an elderly woman (well, she was probably about fifty or sixty years old, but she looked much older) who had weathered skin and no teeth, and was bent over. It turned out this woman had been born on the next farm and had never been farther than the neighboring farm where she had moved after she was married. Those two farms were her whole life. And she was proud of that.

I think I had an appreciation for this Italian tradition of family because I had come from loving parents who had been able to tell me about the lives they had left behind in the old country. Of course, in Turtle Creek most people came from an immigrant background and made a great effort to hold fast to their heritage. So I understood the value of what this old woman had, and I knew that what that little girl lacked in the kind of modern medical care that we had in the States, she made up for in the security of her home and village life.

Often when we were in people's homes, I would be embarrassed by Schuster's lack of appreciation or respect. Oh, he'd warm up when he wanted something; there was almost always a hidden motive.

On the rare occasions when Chuck spoke to me about

his family and growing up in Boston, his description was as vague and rough as an unfinished pencil sketch. From what I could get, it was a dark picture. It seemed to me that in his silences lived the ghosts of many bitter memories. He told me that his interest in body-building had changed his life, giving him purpose and direction. The gym became home, a place where he belonged. He said he worked as a cake decorator to make ends meet, but his real calling was body-building.

As I pieced together Chuck's story, I understood him a little better. Although his tough background likely fostered some of his unsavory ways, it also produced the first-rate warrior he had become.

La Tempesta

The roughest travel was during the time we spent in the mountains, especially on the hike through the most rugged terrain en route to Jesi. One late afternoon when we were walking on a narrow road that was carved into the side of a mountain, about ten kilometers from a small village, thick black clouds slowly swallowed a sickly sun. The wind began an angry howl. With one hand we held our caps on and, with the other, pulled our jackets close around our necks. The falling snow was whipped into wild, whirling cyclones that battered and blinded us. Immediately a great battle raged between us and the blizzard. We'd manage to take two bent-over, staggering steps forward, using all of our strength against the wind, only to be pushed four or five steps backward. At times we feared being blown off the edge of the road into the deep ravine.

Our storms at home were nothing like this. This wind was a vicious thing. It would slam into us hard, harder than you can imagine, as if it hated us. I started to hate it back. We had to lean into it and everything was coming fast. The wind, the snow, the ferocious gusts that stole the very breath from your lungs. Through our travels, we had picked up a few more warm things—some old work-gloves, heavier jackets, a couple of knitted vests—but in this storm our clothes for the most part felt like the thin rags that they were.

We were too busy fighting to stay on our feet to notice the cold. And ignoring the cold was dangerous. That's how guys got bad frostbite and even froze to death. We struggled, clutching each other now, no longer caring about losing our caps. The din of the storm and the force of the wind made speaking and hearing almost impossible. Every so often we did hear a sickening crack as a tree limb gave way. The storm was taking everything. And now the evil darkness of the thing was mixing with the coming night like a witch's brew. We tried to keep as close to the mountain side of the road as possible, clutching at tree limbs and bushes for stability and reassurance that we were not drifting to the outer edge of the road. I prayed for rescue and tried to fight the sense that death was in this storm. This wicked storm seemed to be growing in strength, as ours was seeping away. We had great weights on our feet. Our hands and arms were so cold that we couldn't be sure we were still grasping onto the bushes on the hill side of the road. With every move, I imagined stepping off into nothingness, losing my stomach in the momentary weightlessness.

Finally, I forced myself to hold my breath for a second in order to look up and make sure we were still on the hill side of the road. Fierce tongues of ice and snow burned my skin but I hardly noticed, because something else had caught my attention. It was a light. It was just a short distance up the hill. I grabbed Chuck's arm and pointed. We began hitting each other and pointing. A tiny light. Thank God! We scrambled toward it. Up, up the hill through snowdrifts and ice, frozen bushes, fallen tree branches. Sometimes sliding, sometimes falling. Now we could see the dark outline of a small farmhouse with one small light inside.

We made it to the door, almost falling in as a small weathered man, wearing a nightshirt and carrying a single candle, opened it before we were able to knock. The family had been about to go to bed, he said. But, amazingly, they had heard our approach above the roar of the storm, just before extinguishing the candle. The ice and snow that had covered us was beginning to make great puddles on the farmhouse floor as we realized that we had been saved by looking up at just the right moment, while the candle was still lit. A moment later and it would have been snuffed out for the night…and, for us, forever. I had a fleeting vision of us lying dead and frozen just feet away from the farmhouse.

Now the farmhouse was all bustle as the farmer's wife heated wine for us to drink and the farmer put woven mats on the floor in front of the fire and made a bed of old quilts while his sons put more wood on the fire. After a few crusts of bread and some cheese, the wine did its work and we slept the sleep of the dead with the fire's hot breath engulfing us in oblivion and melting the ice still clinging to the clothes and socks we had hung on a chair.

The next day we awoke with aching hands, feet, legs and joints, and faces glowing from windburn. But we had survived. Incredibly, so had the storm. Although the wind had weakened, a heavy snow had filled in our footprints from the night before, and moody clouds swollen with snow hung overhead.

"You see, you can't think about leaving," the farmer said to us as his wife inspected our still-damp outerwear on the chair in front of the fire. In fact, the long johns we had on under the blankets we had wrapped around us were still damp.

"This storm will be with us through the day at least," the farmer persisted. "Maybe tomorrow you can continue. Maybe the next day. Who knows," he said, making the Italian gesture of shrugging while bending the hand at the wrist, palm upward. I laughed as our host emphasized his uncertainty about the future by gesturing with both hands.

Hearing the farmer's weather prediction, Chuck now became sullen.

That evening we joined the family for roasted rabbit and polenta, which is a sort of cornmeal mush, eaten in true family community. "Mama" put a heavy, well-scrubbed board on the table and spooned the steaming mush onto it in a somewhat flat mound in the center of the board. Then she took a string to section off portions of the polenta and we all gathered around to eat.

With two extra mouths to feed, there wasn't much polenta left over from that meal. But what there was of it was left out overnight to set into a firmer consistency. Then Mama sliced it thick and fried it up for breakfast in a little olive oil. My mouth still waters when I think of it.

I remember on one occasion when our hostess lamented that she only had stale bread to serve us for breakfast. I put the bread on a fork and held it over the fire to toast it lightly. Toast was a new concept to our hosts and soon everyone in the household wanted to have a turn at holding their bread over the fire on a fork to make *"tosta."*

We stayed in the little farmhouse for two nights, with Chuck remaining quiet and sulking over the delay. On the third day, the sky cleared and the wind retreated enough for us to put on our now-stiff boots and fire-roasted outerwear and head out into the morning sun.

Like the thaw that comes with the return of the sun, Chuck's attitude improved, and he was even gracious as the farmer and his family wished us well and sent us off with a small lunch of cheese and bread.

The Mountain Creek

One afternoon we came down into a narrow, deep valley. Here between mountain ranges, the weather, though still cold, was milder than it had been in the higher elevations. After judging by the sun that it was about three or four o'clock, we came to a hilly place where there was a good-sized creek. Along this icy stream, farmers had made a wooden chute that channeled the water down the hill a short distance, where it ran into a big water wheel. We followed a boardwalk running alongside the chute to a house, where we were warmly received.

The farmer, his wife, and children were just about to sit down to their supper. Quickly the farmer ordered the children to bring two more chairs to the table and we sat down to a grand dinner of white pasta followed by roasted pheasant. Many of the families we met depended on wild game as their only source of meat. Being from Western Pennsylvania, I was used to eating rabbit, venison, and birds of all kind, including sparrows. I remember my mother putting chicken feed under a small screen with wooden sides that my father had made for her. She'd prop the screen up delicately with twigs and string and catch herself some sparrows. Then she'd roast them and we'd have a feast that night. When I was older and allowed to roam the woods around Turtle Creek with my friends, we'd catch sparrows, pack them in mud, and bake them for our supper. Now in Italy we were served an array of wild game and even Chuck marveled at the exotic seasonings and culinary techniques of Italian cooks.

This dinner, this roasted pheasant seasoned with wine, garlic and rosemary, pushed us to the limit of our meagre abilities in Italian as we tried to come up with sufficient words of praise for this good hostess and her cooking. We did our best to show our appreciation for her talents. In true Italian fash-

113

ion, she only smiled shyly while her husband beamed and the children giggled.

With our bellies full, sleep that night was good and deep. We set off again in the morning, walking beside the creek. A short distance from the house, the creek went between two steep cliffs. We decided that we didn't want to walk through the water. The day was chilly and overcast, and being wet did not appeal to us. Captain Schuster had an idea. "Let's go up over the hill here and take a shortcut, because this creek looks like it's winding away from us."

I hated to leave that creek, because I knew that any creek or stream would take us into the next valley and eventually to the Adriatic. And now here we were going downhill on the other side of the mountain range away from the creek. You never want to be walking up a creek when you're aiming for the sea. (Maybe that's where the saying comes from—you know, "up the creek.") However, Captain Schuster was the ranking officer, so we went up the hill and walked and walked in order to bypass the creek. Fortunately we had been well fed and we were rested. Even as the day wore on, we were able to keep up a steady pace.

Finally we came to a place where a *contradina* ("farmer") was killing a hog. Some of his neighbors had come by to help with the job. We rested there awhile, and they gave us some food and wine. I was right at home there, having worked all those years in a butcher shop where I kept the fires going in the smokehouse and sampled the sausage. We had a relaxed and happy time with the hog butcher and his friends and went on our way in good cheer.

As evening approached, we came to yet another creek. The landscape looked familiar to me, but I thought maybe I was just getting tired or had had a little too much wine. As we rounded a bend, we both stopped dead in our tracks as we were confronted by the water wheel!

"Oh well," I said, "do you think supper's ready yet?"

When the farmer opened the door, he began laughing, saying, *"Siete putzi!"* ("You're crazy!")

You can bet that the next morning there was no discussion about cutting off that creek.

Chicago Lou

In the foothills of the Apennines on the eastern side of the mountain range, we came to a village on the outskirts of Castiglione. We stopped there in hopes of finding some food and a place to sleep.

As we were talking with some men in an ancient, cave-like *taverna*, a man walked in and came directly over to us. "Americani!" he said in a tone of celebration, and then in practiced English, "You come to my house now for supper, eh? My name is Louis." (He put special emphasis on the "s" in his name, causing his smile to widen.)

"Everyone here calls me Chicago Lou," he explained with a flourish, lingering over the pronunciation of Chicago so that it sounded like Chee-cah-go with the emphasis on the first syllable.

Everything about Chicago Lou was round: his head, his shining brown eyes, his pink cheeks, and a torso shaped like the globe with a belt where the equator would be. He appeared to be in his early forties with thinning black hair and a tiny, perfectly manicured mustache. In fact, this Chicago Lou was well-tended and immaculate, from his expertly ironed white shirt to his gleaming black shoes. His expansive soul was revealed in his perfect smile, featuring even, white teeth no toothpowder advertisement could rival. And Chicago Lou smiled a lot, as he was a truly happy man…and why not!

While two attractive young women served us our dinner of roasted pork and potatoes, Lou talked of his years living on Taylor Street in Chicago's "Little Italy." As a teenager, he had emigrated to the United States with his parents. Both parents died shortly after settling in Chicago. But the enterprising Lou found success in the produce business. He began as a helper to one of his father's distant cousins, an elderly gentleman who had a fruit stand on Maxwell Street in the city's wholesale district. Lou took to the business quickly and learned all he could from his boss. Soon the old man was depending on Lou's energy, youth, and natural intelligence, which allowed him to expand the business. With some winks and flashes of his magnificent smile, Lou implied that while the "expansion" may not have been entirely legal (my guess is that it had something to do with bootlegging), it was wildly successful.

I can still see him nodding his head and rubbing fingers together in the Italian gesture for money as he emphasized that even though the money came pouring in, he was no squanderer. Unlike so many of the era who lost their fortunes on women and gambling, Lou understood the pleasure of quietly socking it away. His financial situation would get even better: when the old man died, having no heirs, he left everything to Lou. Now the orphaned immigrant boy was truly a man of means. But, he reasoned, times were changing in America and Lou had had enough of business (he pronounced it "bus-e-ness") He grew serious as he told us how this "bus-e-ness" was leading to involvement in some dangerous things (or, as he pronounced it, "tings"). He figured that back in Italy his money would buy him a lifetime of security, leisure, and pleasure. Back in Italy he became Chicago Lou, the hometown boy who had made it big in America. Now, with two lovely friends to cook and keep his house clean and his evenings lively, Lou indeed lived a good life.

"So, you two," he said, leaning back in his chair, hands folded on his considerable belly, "stay here with me. I'll fix you up with some nice young women and you can be very happy 'til the war is over, maybe longer. Eh, no more army! No more nothing but good times. What do you say?"

There were at the time a good number of military people on all sides waiting out the war in various circumstances in Italy. There was no doubt that many would remain content and

117

happy to live out their days in this beautiful country long after the war had ended. But we politely thanked Lou and the next morning continued our trek eastward. Although we walked with abundant resolve, I think we both felt just a little wistful at the thought of Lou's attractive offer.

Frank Mauritz

Here I am with my father, Frank,
shortly after I came to live with
the Mauritz's.

Antonia Mauritz

My birth parents, John and Helen Susco, many years after my adoption

My sisters Ann (on left) and Mary with John and Helen Susco

As a schoolboy in Turtle Creek, Pennsylvania

Enjoying the Florida sun before reporting for duty in Texas

As an aviation cadet in Texas

With a fellow cadet in Muskogee

That's me on the far left as a cadet in Muskogee.

Photo by Lt. Basil Blair

Doing what I loved to do best

As an officer in the United States Air Corps shortly before we left for North Africa

With my beautiful new bride, Louise, after the war

Louise and my mother, Antonia

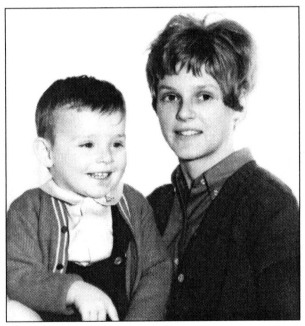

Our children, Craig and Donna, in the 1960s

With two of my four birth sisters and brother, John, in the 1960s

Corporal Larry Schenkel of the United States Rangers

Former Ranger Larry Schenkel in later years

Boyd Fallwell of Oklahoma, that dedicated Honor Guard of one. Fallwell's work so touched my wife's heart that she became a dedicated contributor to his Honor Guard ministry.

Photo by Paolo Varriale

One of the first photos of *Skipper* and the divers after the plane was brought to the surface in January of 1998

Photo by Paolo Varriale

An estimated crowd of 5,000 came to see *Skipper* rescued from Anzio Bay.

131

Skipper as it was displayed upon my arrival at Piana delle Orme Museum. The walls were covered with photographs of the dive and the story of my crash landing in Anzio Bay.

Photo courtesy of Piana delle Orme Museum

Signore de Pasquale standing proudly in front of *Skipper* as it is currently displayed at the Piana delle Orme Museum.

Mariano de Pasquale and I shared the honor of cutting a cake that
bore a perfect replica of *Skipper.*

Dr. Gianni Blasi (far right), a professor of English Literature in Italy, was our first interpreter and served as Master of Ceremonies for several of the lavish events staged by Signore de Pasquale and Piana delle Orme Museum. Dr. Blasi is a true renaissance man.

We rode in Signore de Pasquali's vintage Jeeps when he took us on a tour of his empire.

At lunch with my dear friend, historian Ferdinando d'Amico, the first
to learn who really put *Skipper* down in the bay

I knew d'Amico was a special person when I read his
first letter to me about *Skipper.*

Our great, friend, Diego Cancelli, who also interpreted for us. Diego is smart, funny, kind and, as my daughters say, a hunk.

Donna and Peggy on the beautiful Anzio beach

I was always amazed at the media attention we received at every event and I was honored by the number of people who wanted to talk to me and get my autograph. I understood, however, that I was merely a representative of the thousands who had served in Italy in World War II.

Having Donna, Craig and Peggy share this trip with me was pure joy.

Our guide and interpreter, Diego, made our Roman holiday great fun.

The scenic town of Laterina, location of the prison camp, with the Apennines in the background

The honorable mayor of Laterina held a news conference and a grand luncheon in our honor. (He was a gracious host.)

Signore de Pasquale (right) was always happiest in his
work clothes while overseeing his impressive empire.

I am indebted to Signore d'Amico and Dr. Blasi for their
helpfulness in the writing of this book.

With my cherished friend and fellow soldier, Umberto Capolla, in
Italy in 1998; below, Capolla in military uniform. Doesn't he bear
a striking resemblance to a young Robert De Niro?

Once you've experienced hunger you never forget to thank the cooks, especially these great Italian artists.

Our visit to the Vatican held great symbolism for me

The Fever

Now and then as we got closer to the city of Jesi, we would run into someone who would tell us how the war was going. It was never good. The Nazis were going all out to hold Anzio. Schuster and I both understood that our losses must be great. We were desperate to get back to where we could be of some help to the cause. But I wouldn't let myself fall into the rages of frustration that would overtake Schuster so often. I knew our unit must be right there in the middle of it and I should have been there. I felt as if I had been plucked from the world, the place where I belonged. The road back seemed so long, and I was tired. I had worked hard to train and I loved flying. I felt as though my father had prepared me for this because, above all, he had taught me patience and diligence. Whenever Chuck sank into a black mood because he wanted to get back into the war, I could just see my father giving him a stony look of disapproval. I knew that my father would see this trek as something we had to endure, something we had to get through, and so there was nothing more to say about it.

"Nothing else," Frank Mauritz would say. "You study the problem and get to work solving it. Don't think or do anything else. Take it all in order and stay with it. Stay with it, do what you have to do, and shut up. Then you can work on the next thing. But you never want to get ahead of yourself."

I took this to mean you had to earn your way to the next step. You earned it through work, nothing else.

During the days we walked toward the Adriatic, I knew then more completely than ever before how deeply I loved my father. I guess I am one of those people who can honestly say that my father was the person I most admired. It was true then and it is true now. How I longed to hear his voice and see his face with the light of brilliance in his eyes.

I was so tired. Of course, I knew I was better off here than in a Nazi prison camp. Still, I was haunted by the thought of those guys we left behind. I hoped they hadn't been punished on account of our escaping. When I could remember, I prayed for them. "Dear God, help them and protect them, especially if they've been taken to Germany."

I was sick of the way Chuck took people for granted and thought so little of their kindness.

"I'm going to talk this guy into making me a suit," Chuck said to me one day when we met a young tailor.

"Why?" I answered, disgusted with his foolishness. "How will you pay for it?"

"I have to look better than this! I can get him to do it for me. He'll enjoy telling his friends how he made a suit for a United States Ranger."

I watched him corner this poor fellow, trying to get him to make him some kind of a suit. A suit! We needed to keep going, to get to Ancona, to find a sub. What did he need with a suit? But that was Chuck. He would spend his energies scheming to get something to go his way and if he didn't get what he wanted, he'd rail and finally withdraw in silent despair. His unhappiness, I knew, was a deep and ugly wound. He had been in the thick of it, especially at Anzio where his men had suffered heart-wrenching losses, and he had bled for them. Although he never spoke to me about the circumstances of his capture, I knew it had been brutal.

These experiences on the heels of a painful upbringing seemed to feed his despair. Yet, as the days wore on and I started to put together the little glimpses he had given me of his past, I knew that the best part of his life, the source of his pride, was the time spent in the military as a U. S. Ranger—even taking into account that terrible battle at Anzio and his capture. That was why looking the part was so important to him. His need to get back was a terrible thing sometimes.

I was just so damn tired of it all. The walking, the uncertainty. When you're in a tight spot, it helps to think of things that take you away from your problems and give your mind a break. Right now I was coming up short on that end. I'd try to focus on something and before long, it, too, would turn into something troubling to me. Like my family. I had gotten to the point where I really tried not to think about them or home too much. Whenever I did, my mind would shift to "What did my parents think had happened to me? Did they think I was dead? How were they taking it?" I started to feel as if I was sinking. Sometimes at night I'd look up at the moon and think, "If I could just get up there and hang on for about six hours, I'd be over Pennsylvania and then I could drop down and be home." A lot of things were getting muddled in my head. I could not shake my fears about what happened to the men back in the prison camp after we escaped. And I couldn't bring that up to Chuck. Many of them were his men! But Chuck was a closed door.

Late one afternoon some *Patrioti* brought us to meet a young man, a *patrone*, who they hoped would be willing to feed and house us. While we sat in the kitchen of one of his tenant farmers, I started to shake with cold. My knees were weak and I couldn't keep my eyes open. I was helped into a bed and covered with blankets but I still shook violently. I suppose I slept off and on. I was aware that people were coming into the room where I lay but I couldn't be bothered with them. They tried to warm me by placing a bedwarmer under the covers with me. But I couldn't open my eyes and I was still shaking with cold. Sometime after that, I don't know how long, I started sweating. I remember waking up and finding the *patrone* in the room. He spoke to me but I didn't understand him. I can't tell you if days or hours had passed. And then the *patrone* went away.

My chest felt as though someone was sitting on it. And my side hurt, too. I was now very hot. People would wake me and give me little sips of water and then I would sleep. I remember their rolling me to one side so that they could put dry sheets on the bed, then rolling me to the other side to finish the job. (I later learned that they had to change my sweat-soaked sheets twice a day!) The *patrone* came and went. People came into my room. Sometimes I thought my father was there, sitting beside my bed. Once I heard my mother talking to him but I couldn't see her. At other times I was in the cockpit. I'd reach for things, try to see the dials and instruments, but nothing ever made sense. I'd try to look out and see where I was flying but I couldn't see anything. I knew days were passing but I don't know how I knew. I just wanted to sleep.

One day—it was late afternoon by the sun—I woke up more fully that I had in many days. I heard Chuck Schuster's voice and I called to him. When he walked into the room, I asked, "What's happened to me?"

"You have pneumonia," he answered. "Looks like your fever's broken. They said if that happened you'd probably be okay."

"How long have I been sick?"

"About a week," he told me. Chuck had been staying in another house some distance away. "When you got real bad, Marcantonio got you some kind of medicine. I guess it worked."

Angelo Marcantonio was the young *patrone* who owned the farm where I was staying as well as several other farms in the vicinity. When we arrived here, Signore Marcantonio was the *patrone* who had agreed to help us.

But a week! A week had passed. How could it be that long? But when I tried to lift myself, I had no strength. It must be true. And, incredibly, Chuck had stayed. He waited for me. After all of his tirades about moving faster, getting to Ancona, finding the subs, never getting bogged down! And he continued to wait over the next week as I regained my appetite and strength.

The family who cared for me were the Alessios: Maria, Vincenzo, and their daughters. Signora Alessio kept a constant stream of her good soup coming my way. Vincenzo, the tenant farmer, provided the wild game and chickens that went into the soup. And the Alessio daughters washed my damp bed linens and waved to me from the other room, as it was not thought appropriate for young, unmarried women to tend to a young man who was sick in bed.

Sometimes in the evening Vincenzo would sit with me. He had a great interest in America and how we lived there. One evening he listened with fascination as I explained and sketched out our system of central heating. Our good old coal furnace was a wonder to Vincenzo.

But the real wonder was the family themselves. All that time nursing me, they were in great danger of being caught. The longer I stayed with them, the more difficult it became to keep my presence a secret. They had risked everything to keep me alive. What nobility! What great giving spirits they had!

Finally I felt strong enough to get back on the road. But as Chuck and I prepared to leave, Vincenzo called us aside and pressed some money into Chuck's hand. He placed his finger alongside his nose, the Italian signal for secrecy, and said simply, "It might be smarter for you two to take a bus to the coast."

We assumed the money had come from the *patrone*, Signore Marcantonio. Vincenzo didn't say, and we didn't ask.

"*Grazie! grazie!*" was all we could say. After many hugs and handshakes, we gave them our chits and were off.

Now Chuck was as happy as I had ever seen him. We were going to make up for time lost and be in Ancona within a day!

But these people. These Italians. There was something different about them. I mean, they took such pride in their giving and helping. Back home I had seen generosity, especially during the Depression, but even my father gave with a certain seriousness. I think his attitude was that he felt duty-bound to help and, being a man of honor and good character, help he did, but always with the attitude that his aid should serve to get the needy person back on the road to self-sufficiency. As for other people in our church and our town, their giving had a kind of grimness or burden to it. Maybe I'm being harsh, but I think that, compared to the Italians that I met, their generosity showed little heart and no joy. Everyone should be blessed with the gift the Italians have for giving, a gift of love and warmth and joy in helping. They made you think it was their greatest pleasure to help. Grace, graciousness, I guess that's what we were experiencing, and it was grand.

The Autobus

In a small town a few miles from where Signore Marcantonio and the Alessios lived, we stood at the bus stop trying to look inconspicuous. Suddenly from around the corner of a building came a man in a uniform. An Italian in uniform. *Fascista!* Damn! Nothing could be worse than the *Fascisti*.

Germans could walk right past us and never realize that we weren't Italians. We had made this happy discovery while we were on the road outside of Jesi. Knowing that there was an air field in the area, we were entertaining ourselves with talk about how terrific it would be to steal a plane and how I could fly us back behind the lines. The plan was as far-fetched as my flying to the moon, but it passed the time.

So we were chewing the fat this way as we emerged on the other side of a thick wood and headed down a road. Suddenly from around the bend we heard the unmistakably German "Hup! Hup! Hup!" and the sound of boots in a march step. Chuck and I knew that running was out of the question. It was too late for that anyway. A few more paces—a mere heartbeat—and they were in sight. We could do nothing but maintain our composure and stay where we were. When you're engaged in a deception, seconds can seem like hours. During that time you hold your breath while trying to look like you're breathing normally. You feel frozen and wooden just when you want to appear loose and casual. So there we were, when, to our amazement, a detail of about twelve of them passed us—"Hup! Hup! Hup!" They went right by us as though we were invisible or of no consequence, just two Italian men heading into town. Two locals, dirty and poor. We didn't speak or turn around for a good long while, for fear that someone was watching or might even be following this group. But as we put distance between them and us, I felt the fear and tension drain from me and I could sense the same thing happening to Chuck.

The area through which we were traveling was thick with German officers who were being sent to a rest camp. The group we saw being marched along were likely the men assigned to serve the officers at the camp.

Even though we had to continue to be careful, we both took some comfort in knowing we could pass ourselves off as Italians to the Germans. The Italians were a different story. All too often we were approached by friendly Italians saying, *"'mericani? Inglese? Scapati, si?"* I guess you know your own so well you can easily spot one who isn't. Something about us was all too obvious to the Italians. Maybe it was our height, our manner, or the way we walked. Whatever it was, the Italians were always able to read us loud and clear.

That is why we knew that the Italian in uniform waiting for the bus could mean serious trouble for us. We couldn't tell if he was armed. Would he think *we* were armed? Would there be more coming? We couldn't tell if he was police, military, or military police. He looked at us for what seemed like too long a time. Then he looked away, but he had stopped walking and stood too close to us for Chuck and me to chance speaking to each other. It looked as if he, too, was waiting for the damn bus.

After about fifteen minutes, a battered bus with most of its paint gone rocked into view, carrying boxes, furniture, and even a crate of chickens on its roof. It labored to an exhausted stop with an almost audible sigh. Four or five people got off. The Italian in uniform got on the bus through the back door, and Chuck and I boarded through the front door. The bus was crowded. Even standing room was tight. We were thankful that we could stay near the front, and away from the uniformed man. Occasionally one of us would sneak a glance back at him and see that he was straining to keep us in sight. Although we couldn't discuss it, we both feared that he might be meeting his comrades in Ancona or anywhere en route.

It had been a long time since either of us had traveled in any normal mode. It might have been childish of me, but I had been looking forward to a bus ride. I imagined that we could just slump down in our seats and watch the countryside slip by. And I guess I needed to let down my guard for a little while. Hell, I just wanted to sit back and let the world go by without having to keep my antennae up. Even standing would have been pleasant without that guy in the uniform eyeing us. But there he was and we didn't know what it was going to mean to us.

When the bus stopped in a small village, we glanced back to see if the man got off. He didn't. I looked at Chuck to see if he thought we should get off, but he whispered, "Stay put," and I agreed. This was our opportunity at last to get to Ancona. We had worked too hard to get there. I figured Chuck was thinking we'd stand a good chance of ditching the man in the crowds in Ancona. I also drew some strange comfort from knowing that he wouldn't hesitate to lure the man into a back alley and kill him if it became necessary.

You see, I was a hypocrite then and I still am. I hated the killing. All of it. I know that death from a bomb dropped on human beings is the same as murdering them by snapping their necks. It's all killing. Like many who fought this war or any war, I hated it, even as I understood it to be my duty. Time and again I prayed I was only destroying property. As a fighter pilot I had the luxury of not really knowing what human damage I might have inflicted. But regardless of my own convictions, I couldn't judge Chuck. We needed people like him who could do it face to face (so close they could smell the guy), who could stand to see the fellow die, who could feel the life leave his body and somehow live with it. Hell, it was all so mixed up. All you could do was hope and pray to God you were doing the right thing moment to moment.

After a rough and tense ride we finally arrived in Ancona. Everyone crowded off the bus and we stayed with the swell, heading down the street, trying to look as though we knew where we were going. We couldn't turn and look directly at the man in uniform, but as best as we could tell it didn't seem that he was following us. After walking several more blocks we passed a man in a suit who gave us an odd look. A little farther down the street we became aware that *that man* was following us! What a helluva day we were having!

As we had expected, the streets of Ancona were crowded with people. But we would turn down a side street thinking we had lost our man when, sure enough, there he was, craning his neck to see us over the crowd. We would speed up and he would speed up.

"This guy," Chuck muttered under his breath as we walked quickly down a narrow street, with the man about a block behind us, "I don't think we're gonna be able to ditch him."

"We gotta get inside somewhere," I said, hoping to avoid a confrontation with our pursuer. "Let's just try a door. You with me?"

"Go ahead," he said, to my great relief.

So we did what we had never done before: we tried the door latch of a private home, found it opened, and ducked inside without knocking.

There was no entry hall in this house. The door simply opened into what appeared to be the main room. It's a funny thing when you do something like that without having any idea of what you're going to find. You're focused on getting away from what's outside, so your attention doesn't shift right away to what you've stepped into. For a second or two after we slipped into the darkness of the house, we weren't aware of our surroundings. That took maybe a heartbeat or so. When it did come into focus, we were dumbfounded as our brains shifted gears and allowed us to grasp the fact that we were right in the middle of a wake! There in one corner of the room, on a couch, lay a small bald man dressed, apparently, in his Sunday best. Four or five women in black sat nearest the deceased with a dozen or so men and children forming a kind of outer circle of mourners. The shutters were closed, keeping the room very dark, with only a few candles or small lamps lit near the dead man.

Now all heads had turned from the deceased to us. I heard words of exclamation, but I didn't know what they were saying. Although we were standing in relative darkness, it was apparently obvious to the mourners that we didn't belong there. *"Pardona, pardona, 'scusati!"* we began saying as the men approached us. I don't remember if they were saying anything to us, but they didn't seem in any way hostile, just curious. As we began explaining our situation and telling them that we thought we were being followed, they became sympathetic and welcoming.

Suddenly the door opened and in walked the man in the suit! Schuster and I froze as the man, red-faced, eyes bulging, began shouting something at the top of his voice. He walked right over to us and continued his tirade while the mourners, who had, for the moment, forgotten all about the deceased, gathered around us and listened with great interest.

After a time, we began to understand that he was trying to tell us that we had put ourselves in great danger by walking past a police station. He said that he knew right away that we were English or American. He told us that we looked too obvious and that there were many dangers in Ancona.

We had learned a thing or two about Italians during our time in Italy. One of them was that an Italian who is merely trying to explain something important to you might do so at the top of his lungs, as close as possible to your face, with all of the hand and arm gestures of a New York City traffic cop. Until you have a grasp of the language and the culture, you could begin to think the whole encounter was going to end in physical violence of some sort. (In this case, however, the man was considerably smaller than either Schuster, the former weightlifter, or I.) But when you know a little of the language and you have survived a few of these exchanges, you realize that this is merely mannerism and posturing for emphasis. In Italy, talking can be, and often is, a physical activity involving the entire body. When the speakers feel that they have made their point, the mood switches with lightning speed and all parties are once again amiable and polite.

As soon as the gentleman in the suit was assured by us and the mourners (who seemed to have absorbed us into their inner circle) that no further risks would be taken, he made a remarkable change in his manner. He stepped back, took a deep breath, produced a clean handkerchief, patted his damp brow, returned the handkerchief, smoothed his hair, straightened his tie and, with his dignity collected, offered his condolences to the mourners, going round the circle of them, one by one. Then he wished us well, shook hands all around again, and left.

Ancona

We spent several days in the busy seaport town of Ancona. The family of the deceased had arranged to put us up in separate houses. Although people did confirm that British subs had been in the Adriatic picking up escapees, all agreed that none had been there in recent weeks. The Allies were still pinned down at Anzio. And just as the man in the suit had warned, Ancona was a haven for Fascists and sympathizers. As desperate as Chuck was to get back to the business of war, even he saw the danger in waiting it out in Ancona. So we agreed to leave the city.

This was not an easy decision. For such a long time we had kept Ancona and the subs in our minds as our great hope of getting back. Many nights I dreamed of those British subs, imagining that I could see one out on the horizon. It would be just a silhouette against the sky, and the sky would be the soft pink it gets just before dawn. I knew it would surface magnificently from the depths of the Adriatic. And Chuck and I would swim out to it. In my dreams we never made it all the way, but the swimming was fast and easy and it always seemed that we were going to make it and everything was going to be good. Then I'd wake up in some barn or in a strange bed or on a floor somewhere and we'd press on toward Ancona. Now we were leaving Ancona and the promise of rescue.

For a time we traveled southward, staying off the winding main roads. We passed the outskirts of the city of Osimo. People now warned us constantly of the heavy presence of Germans. So we kept to the country roads and sometimes even walked through the woods, keeping a road or a stream in view. On the outskirts of the town of Loreto we came to a river, the Musone, I believe. Because all of the bridges were guarded by

Nazis or *Fascisti*, we had to find a spot where we could wade across. When we reached an area that looked rocky but shallow, Chuck sat down and began unlacing his boots.

"You're taking your boots off?" I asked.

"It'll take too long for them to dry out. And I hate like hell walking in wet boots. Not good for the feet."

Remembering how I had suffered with stiff, swollen feet at the beginning of our walk, I was soon unlacing my own boots. At first it seemed Chuck had been right. The water wasn't unbearably cold and the walking was easy, but as we got into the middle, the rocks became sharper and more slippery. Now we had to walk very slowly to avoid slipping. With each step the uneven rocks jabbed and sliced at our feet. I imagined the river filling with streaks of blood from our wounds but I couldn't make myself look down, because I was too intent upon watching the banks for sharpshooters. We were easy targets out there in that river, picking our way across.

The pain didn't start until we had dried our feet and put our socks and boots back on. Then, walking with all of those abrasions throbbing was a hell of the worst kind. With every step I whispered, correctly or incorrectly, every rich and glorious Italian cuss word I had ever heard. For this sort of agony, English wasn't near good enough.

After that river crossing we laid up for a few days with a farmer and let our feet heal before starting off again.

But we weren't through with rivers yet. Several days later when we were approaching what, if I remember correctly, was the Potenza River, we faced another challenge. We were within sight of a bridge known to be guarded by Germans.

"Let's go up there around that bend," I suggested to Chuck.

"Too far," he said. "I think we can get across right here without them seeing us. There's enough brush to cover us. We won't be out in the open all that long."

Once again I had to remind myself that he was the rank-

157

ing officer and so, against my better judgment, I agreed to try it
...this time with my boots *on.*

Again it went well until we got to the middle. Then I
heard "Crack!" and saw the water dimple just ahead and to the
side of me. Again, "Crack! crack! crack!" They were shooting
at us!

It was like another of those bad dreams when you're trying to run, but can only go slowly because you're so weighted
down. I thought back to that damp field where the clumps of
soil stuck to our boots as we escaped from the prison camp at
Laterina. Our situation in this river was far worse. The water
was just above our knees and we couldn't get any speed.

"Crack! crack! crack!" They kept after us, probably
enjoying the sport. Somehow we managed to stay out of their
range, and when we reached the other side the firing stopped.
We scrambled up the bank and didn't stop until we were well
out of sight of the guards.

I resolved that, from here on, I would no longer defer to
the Captain. I was also anxious to get back, but alive!

Chuck had once more demonstrated to me that his judgment was off. We had taken a stupid risk and he had known it
at the time—but then, so did I. I should have stuck to my guns.
I should have known that he had probably been yearning for a
little action and danger. That was probably it. I should have
known you could never be certain of anything with Chuck. And
the time would come when he would demonstrate that on a
grander scale.

Our Friend Caesare

One windy and cold day Chuck and I walked in silence until we came to a tiny tavern where we were treated to a dinner of roasted sausages and peppers. The tavern owner let us sleep in the back room, and the next day, while we were having our morning coffee (and it was actually coffee!), an invitation arrived.

A powerful landowner had learned of our presence and was inviting us to what he proposed would be a real American dinner. It seems this gentleman had spent a good deal of time in the States—*"New York-a Cee-tee,"* the tavern owner told us with pride. So late in the afternoon an old man, in an even older pick-up truck, called for us and took us to the home of Caesare Angelasante. Our driver explained that Signore Angelasante was the *patrone*, owning all of the farmland and vineyards in the area.

It was evening as we approached, and we marveled at our first sight of the elegant Casa de Angelasante sitting on a hilltop. But as we got closer to the grand old villa, the crumbling stucco, rotted shutters, and gaps in the wrought iron of the second-story balconies brought the war into focus. It wasn't only the bombs and shells that left scars. A collapsed economy and chronic shortages contributed to the ruin.

Once inside, our driver led us to an upstairs sitting room and told us that Don Caesare would be with us momentarily. Then he left us to explore the room, a room that had apparently lived many lives. The vaulted ceilings and floor-to-ceiling, balconied windows put me in mind of a ballroom. An ornately carved monster of a table with legs as thick as an elephant's was surrounded by fourteen matching chairs which, along with the china closet, gave the room the appearance of a dining room. But now the table was covered with papers, filled ashtrays, books, maps, and cartons of something stacked nearly to the ceiling. The china closet held additional books and ledgers as well as a few bottles of liquor. Lining one wall were couches and gilded chairs in a variety of fabrics and styles, each one faded, sagging, and worn. My mother would have declared this house, in its day, or at least this room, to be "veddy, veddy fency." But in its present condition she would have clucked her disapproval at the clutter and the undisturbed dust and cobwebs.

Schuster busied himself studying the large map that was hanging on the wall and nearly covering a peeling and faded fresco. He pointed out that our host was tracking Allied troop movements with colored pins that indicated the front and those Italian cities that had been liberated. If Signore Angelasante's map was accurate, the front had moved a little farther north. But only a little.

Finally Caesare Angelasante himself entered the room. He was tall and lean and looked to be in his early forties with thinning, light brown hair and bright blue eyes. He had a generous smile and he shook our hands with great enthusiasm. In English he said, "So you are the two who walked from Laterina! You must be pretty tough to make it over the mountains in winter. You like my map there? You can see the Allies are doing a little better now. But," he added, laughing benevolently, "you two are still in big trouble here in my neighborhood."

"Is your information current and accurate?" Schuster asked.

"Accurate? But of course it is accurate. My sources are the best. How about a drink? Cognac, anisette? Would you like a cigarette or cigar? Enzo!" he called to the driver, who appeared in an instant through one of the many doorways, "bring some glasses. Cognac? Okay!" he smiled, taking great pleasure in his command of our language.

Not to be outdone, Schuster answered, "*Si, cognac piacere.*"

Cognac was more than okay with me. We settled back

and listened to our pleasant and talkative host describe his position as he puffed on a cigar and sipped his cognac with his long legs stretched out in front of him.

From the moment Schuster had expressed his desire for cognac in Italian, our host had nodded his appreciation and switched languages. Now speaking mainly to Chuck in Italian with a few English words thrown in, Caesare explained that although he supported the Allies he also maintained a friendly relationship with the Germans and was, in fact, entertaining them that very evening downstairs!

"They're waiting down there now," he said, laughing and thoroughly enjoying the wary look on our faces. Then he added, in English for my benefit, "You probably walked right past the door to my parlor where they're drinking up my best brandy, I'll wager."

Had we walked into a trap? Chuck and I shot each other a look as our host explained that his comfortable relationship with the Germans made it possible for him to receive mail from his relatives in southern Italy and to get a little gasoline from time to time.

"But you must understand that I am no *Fascista* and no friend of the Nazis." Poking his finger into the air, he continued, "But I am no bastard Communist either! I am my own man and a damn good businessman. I believe Italy will prosper when it is united and rid of the invaders." Then, with his smile returning, he added, "We must be Italian!", speaking very in slowly in English and emphasizing each syllable of "Italian" so that it sounded like "Eee-tahl-yahn."

"I'm betting on your side," Angelasante said in English, leaning forward and looking intently at both of us. "If the war goes your way—and it will—Italy will benefit and so will I. I've been able to do some favors for these Germans in order to get what I needed. But," he continued speaking slowly for emphasis, "I have given them nothing of importance—nothing that aided their cause—only their comfort. You understand what I'm saying?"

I was beginning to like this Angelasante fellow and he clearly liked us and our country. He loved talking about his experience in America, though he never answered us when we asked why he had been there in the first place.

"New York City is best of all. Beautiful women everywhere, like heaven! Big money in that city, you know. After the war I might go back—just to visit."

Before excusing himself to go and entertain his German friends downstairs, our host called for his driver, saying, "Enzo, I think these gentlemen must be ready for dinner." Then turning to us he said, "I insist that you spend the night here," indicating a bedroom on the other side of the hall. "I personally guarantee your safety. What do you say?"

I didn't think we would be any better off leaving the villa at that hour. After all, if our host was going to turn us over to the Nazis, he could just as well do it the moment we stepped outside. And truthfully, I believed Caesare Angelasante was no Nazi collaborator. When I looked at Chuck I could tell he had come to the same conclusion.

Before very long the faithful Enzo came back into the room, carrying a large tray covered with a white cloth. Now the room filled with a wonderful aroma! It smelled like home! Or was it just my imagination? Angelasante beamed as the driver set the tray down on the table. Like a magician, he pulled the cloth from the tray with a flourish and there before us was a loaf of fresh bread, a bottle of wine, and a large platter of ham 'n' eggs.

"*Buon appetito!*" Signore Angelasante said with a smile. And in English, "See what I learned in Aah-mer-ee-ca! You can tell 'em in New York, 'Angelasante doesn't forget!' *Buonanotte*, Yanks!", and he was gone.

That night, looking at Caesare's map, Chuck and I decided to go farther westward, away from the coast and its dangers. We planned to head inland and then south, where we hoped to meet up with the Allies.

When we told Angelasante our plan the next morning, he agreed that we were wise to get away from the heavily populated Adriatic coast. And he said he had a plan. After a word to his driver, we were presented with two bicycles.

In Italian, Angelasante said, "You'll make better time and look more like Italians using these. But," he warned, "you have to ride like Italians and not like Americans."

For a minute I thought he was joking. But then he demonstrated with his hands, explaining that Americans, accustomed to foot brakes, coast downhill on a European bicycle holding the pedals level as if to slow the bike. Italians, knowing that the pedals have no function in breaking, leave them in an uneven position. He feared we would give ourselves away if we coasted downhill our customary way.

"Now, you follow Enzo. Not too close but keep him in sight. He'll take you to a *Patrioti* village. You can trust Enzo, he is a *Patrioto* to the bone, eh, Enzo?" he said, patting him on the back. "And you can trust me, too. Angelasante wants to make sure you guys get back to all those beautiful women in New York!"

We said our goodbyes to Signore Angelasante, who refused our chits. "No, no, you were my guests. Now, watch your feet on those bicycles."

We agreed to be mindful of our feet and off we went, following at a safe distance while keeping Enzo's bicycle in sight.

By nightfall we arrived in a mountain village where Enzo took us quickly to a house near the outskirts. After brief introductions were made and the door was latched behind us, the owner of the house pulled a table aside, threw back a piece of carpet, and opened a trapdoor leading to a basement. "My friends are down here. They'll be happy to help you."

In the basement were five young men sitting on cartons, eating salami and bread. The owner of the house presented us to the group and told them about our situation. He then explained to us that these five were members of the Italian Resistance, the *Patrioti.*

While they talked over their evening meal, I did the best I could to follow their conversation. I leaned over to Chuck. "Am I getting this right? They're planning to head farther up into the mountains?"

"Yeah. It might be a few days before they're ready, but they're willing to take us with them. So it looks like we'll be here for a while."

Joining them seemed like a good idea to me, and I was relieved to see that Chuck agreed. When we awoke the next morning, Enzo and all five of the young *Patrioti* were gone. The owner of the house explained that Enzo had returned to Signore Angelasante but that the *Patrioti* had gone off long before dawn and would probably be back before nightfall. Shortly after dark, there was a light tapping on the door and all five slipped quickly into the house and down into the basement like wary rodents. This time they were speaking so low and quickly that even Chuck had a hard time following. In the end we understood that we would be leaving for a mountain village before dawn. It was on that frigid morning that we learned just how resourceful this daring band of underground fighters could be.

A Dangerous Truck Ride

The *Patrioti* had stolen a Fascist truck that had *"Grano per il Vaticano"* ("Wheat for the Vatican") painted on its side. Until we climbed in and actually saw sacks of wheat, we thought the sign might have been a clever cover for the *Patrioti*. We didn't ask how they had stolen the truck or what had become of the drivers. But the canvas-covered bed would serve us well for our trip west into the Apennines and our return to the safety of the snow.

This Italian underground was a ragtag lot, unwashed, undisciplined, and unafraid. They inflicted damage and destruction wherever they could in order to thwart the *Fascisti* and the Nazis. If caught, they would face death by torture. But they had gambled on the Allies pushing forward and liberating Italy before they could be captured. They were committed to doing all they could to ensure the success of the Allied push northward.

Two *Patrioti* rode in the cab of the truck, one driving in typical heart-stopping Italian fashion on the twisted and muddy mountain roads, while the other rode shotgun. Three other Italians rode in the back with us on sacks of wheat. Two of the men were armed, but the third was not. The higher we climbed, the colder it got in the back of the truck.

After a while I rolled a cigarette, and then noticed that the unarmed Italian looked rather dejected. So I offered him a smoke. But before he had an opportunity to respond, one of the armed Italians vehemently objected, *"No! No sigaretta per questo bastardo!"*

Bastard? What was he talking about? *"Perche?"* I asked. Why?

The *Patrioto* explained that the man was their prisoner. He had been secretary to the top Fascist in that area. They were planning to exchange him for some of their friends who were being held prisoner by the *Fascisti*.

"All the more reason this poor man should have a smoke if he wished," I thought, and argued on his behalf that one cigarette was nothing but a small civility. What would it hurt to be a little kind? As it turned out, the *Patrioto* who had shouted at me was a compassionate fellow. After pausing for a moment to consider, he motioned to me that he would allow the prisoner to have a smoke.

We were still enjoying our smokes when suddenly, "POW! POW! POW!" Gunfire tore a hole in the canvas just across from me, meaning that bullets had just missed my head! The truck slammed to a halt. The radiator hissed loudly under a barrage of bullets. Now the truck emptied out and there was a great deal of yelling, swearing, and utter confusion as *Patrioti* confronted *Patrioti*. Surely all human beings become emotional when they're upset or scared, but Italians do it with more energy and intensity. They respond in an explosion of words, sounds, and gestures. One would expect them to come to blows but, amazingly, most of the time, they don't. And this time fortunately was no exception. It seems we had run into an ambush set up by the *Patrioti*, who didn't recognize their fellow partisans in the stolen truck. In the end the ruined truck was abandoned and we all set off on foot. Some of them continued cursing their fellow terrorists, calling them *brutti! stupidi!* and worse…much worse.

After hours of walking we came to a small village not far from Macerata. We were now back in the region of Tuscany. The *Patrioti* explained to us that this entire village was partisan and therefore safe. The village was set in a valley that even in late winter had a lush beauty. The little stucco houses were nestled close to one another; although they had suffered no battle damage, they still bore evidence of the effects of the long war in the peeling, faded paint and unrepaired earthquake cracks.

But as we approached, smiling villagers greeted us with

sunny enthusiasm. We were struck by the great number of children and were told that many were brought here for safety after their parents had been killed or imprisoned by the *Fascisti* and Nazis. Among those who came to welcome us was a tall, handsome, middle-aged woman who wore her blond hair in braids wound around her head. She reminded me of pictures my mother had shown me of her family back in the old country in Sarajevo. When the woman was introduced to us, I was surprised to learn that she was Russian. As best as Chuck and I could understand, she had been taken prisoner by the Nazis and brought to Italy to be a servant to them. She had somehow managed to escape her captors and made her way to this partisan village where she settled in quite happily, taking care of the orphaned children, cooking, and baking bread. She apparently spoke fluent Italian with what I presumed was a heavy Russian accent.

War does a lot of things but most of all it changes and wrecks lives and mixes people up so that they end up all over the place. Once we ran into four Serbs in Italy, high in the mountains. They had been hiding from the Germans, waiting out the war in Italy. We also ran into some French doing the same thing. That's war.

This Russian woman was happy to be alive and to have her freedom, but she had her heartaches, too. She told us that she had been married to a man who got drafted into the Russian army, but that she had not seen or heard from him since her capture many years ago. She said she had to accept the fact that he may be dead by now.

As horrible as war is, good can come out of it. This woman, for example, had apparently lost everything and had been taken from everything she had known. God knows what horrors she suffered at the hands of the Nazis. But not only was she welcomed into this little Italian village, she found a useful and meaningful life for herself taking care of the children. And those children were truly blessed to have her. Not such a bad fate.

The longer I was with Chuck Schuster, the more clearly

I could see that he had no interest in the human side of this war. He was obsessed with getting back into the fray, and that obsession seemed to blind him to the goodness and blessings that had followed us on our journey.

Once, while we were spending the night in a farmhouse, our host insisted that we drink anisette with him and asked us to wait while he walked into the village to get some. When he returned, red-faced from the long walk in the cold, he pulled a bottle out of his shirt, put it gently down on the table, and delicately poured out three glasses. After an evening of many toasts, our host was snoring in his bed, and Schuster and I were happily doing the same by the fire. The next morning, when I remarked on our friend's extravagant act of generosity, Schuster's only comment was that the liquor had not been of very good quality.

Back to the High Country

During our stay in the village near Macerata, we came to know a handsome, official-looking, young Italian gentleman who seemed to be in charge. Unlike the ragged, reckless, and undisciplined *Patrioti* in our little band, this young man was immaculately turned out in full military attire, of a sort. He appeared to be about thirty, with a classic Roman profile, and was known respectfully as "the lieutenant." He sported a red satin sash around his waist and wore high, spit-shined boots which may have been stolen from a dead Nazi. Despite his formal, authoritative bearing, he was clearly loved by the villagers whom he treated with kindness and gentleness.

It was the lieutenant who announced to us that the village was no longer safe. I never learned how he got his information, but it was decided that all of us—some fifty men, women, and children from the village, the *Patrioti,* Schuster, and I—should move up into the higher altitudes where the snow was still heavy enough to shield us from the Nazi presence.

As we traveled, the lieutenant walked up and down the column we had formed, making sure that everyone was managing the climb. He was especially concerned about the elderly villagers and looked after each one with great care.

Toward nightfall we came to a tiny settlement that clung to the very edge of a cliff. The snows here were heavy and deep and the air was thin and bitter cold. It was an ideal hideout; from the outermost edge of the cliff, you could see the road to Fabriano, where the Nazis were entrenched. Anyone approaching would be seen in plenty of time for us to attack or flee.

Before we settled in, Schuster and I were introduced to two South African sergeant-majors who had been staying in the mountain hideout for some weeks. Both had been serving in Italy a long while and both spoke fluent Italian. The two, who were white South Africans, had been working closely with the *Patrioti* and were highly regarded by them and the Italian lieutenant.

As the days passed, some of our restless, young *Patrioti* occasionally ventured down the mountainside to harass the Germans and steal from them, but for the most part, we kept to ourselves and managed to make do with what was available.

The *Patrioti* had established radio contact with the British. Occasionally the Brits would send a twin-engine plane overhead to drop supplies to us. We would build three fires in a triangular formation so that they would know where to make the drop. The dropped packages contained all manner of food and medical supplies, probably whatever the Brits could collect. There would be rations from the U. S. military, food in tins from Canada, and one of my favorites—orange marmalade from Australia.

Late one evening the plane made its drop in our triangle, but as it flew off we could hear one of the engines making a terrible noise. Our stomachs turned as we watched flames shoot out of the plane. As the plane went out of view there was a loud booming sound and then silence. We prayed that the crew had bailed out safely. We could do nothing in the darkness. But back in the village, we spent a restless night. At first light, everyone who could walk, or had shoes that could manage the deep, frozen snow, went in search of the crew. Mercifully, we didn't have to walk far before we saw five figures struggling toward us. All were uninjured, except for one poor fellow who had lost his boots and had been trudging in the snow all night in stockinged feet! So now we added five more to our little family up on the mountain.

And family we had become. A rather big family. There were, of course, the *Patrioti*, the two South Africans, the children, the Russian woman, the villagers, the village priest, Padre Gaspare (an Italian priest with, believe it or not, a Scottish

brogue), even the *Fascista* prisoner, all under the care and protection of the lieutenant. The younger women who had been
evacuated with us did the cooking, and we all ate our meals as
a community. We often passed the time by playing cards.

Also included in our mountain village family was an
English artillery captain. His name was Charles Bender.

Ben, as we called him, had been held by the *Fascisti* in
a prison camp in Northern Italy for two years. He was released
when Italy capitulated. The captain, who had arrived shortly
before we did, had made his way to our mountaintop on foot
with the aid of the *Patrioti*. Although his experience as both
prisoner of war and "evadee" had been difficult, Ben always
dismissed his ordeal as part of the job.

He was stocky, with thinning blond hair and a perpetual
flush. He cherished his pipe and, during times of stress or deep
contemplation, would hold it between his teeth or carry it in his
hand even when he had no tobacco. When Ben was lucky
enough to get some tobacco, he would walk around for days
puffing prudently on his filled but unlit pipe, happy to enjoy the
mere aroma of the precious stuff. That was key to Ben's per-
sonality. He could make do with very little and be happy and
grateful for any bit of pleasure or comfort—a sliver of soap, a
little honey for his tea, the luxury of tea itself. He always found
the good in situations, and when even that was in short supply
he maintained his civility. It was a matter of pride with him.

Ben was a master bridge player, and though I had no
experience he patiently taught me the intricacies of the game.
He loved a good joke in the dry manner of his countrymen. His
crisp English accent was music to my ears. When you have to
struggle to understand and to be understood in a foreign country, it is a relief to converse in your native tongue, especially
with someone who is a good conversationalist.

Ben and I were enormously entertained by our chats
with Padre Gaspare. The good man was anxious to practice
speaking his English, which he had learned from two Scottish

soldiers who had passed through his village early in the war. He was extremely proud of his English, though his heavy Italian accent laced with a Scottish brogue often defied comprehension.

"'Tis very good, laddie" would come from Padre Gaspare's Italian lips as "Tees var-ee gude-a, lettia." For a long time, Ben and I were massively confused by the padre's reference to us as "lattiazee." He would say, for example, "So you fen-cee the marmelatee, lattiazee?", or "Come, lattiazee, seat with me." At last we realized he was saying, "So you fancy the marmalade, laddies?" Apparently he was pluralizing laddies, which he pronounced "lettia" in the singular. A cow, which in Italian is *"vacca,"* became a "cooo" in the padre's English. But best of all, Padre Gaspare, earnest as he was about learning English, was never offended when Ben and I would laugh our *arses* off as he tortured and twisted the language with his English-Italian brogue.

Ben also had some fun with our American English. When one of us would say, for example, "I gotta take a leak," Ben would never fail to say, "Aw, come now, Yank, why don't you just leave it there, why take it with you?"

Ben seemed to understand immediately how to get on with Chuck. He would sit quietly while Chuck boasted of his war experiences. When Chuck would rage about the urgency of his getting back into action, Ben would simply say, "Look, it's no good carping, Chuck. If you get yourself recaptured or killed taking foolish risks, you'll do no good a'tall."

He was grateful to the *Patrioti* and shared my admiration for Italian generosity. I felt lucky to have run into the likes of Charles Bender, but in the coming months I would learn that our meeting was fortuitous for other, more serious reasons.

La Primavera

As the weeks passed, the change of season began to unfold. The snowbanks were disappearing and the earth was beginning to smell of that first awakening dampness. Soon the pathways were slushy and everything was dripping wet. It was time to move on.

With great efficiency, the lieutenant organized his villagers and soon we were all ready to trudge down from the high country. The roads were muddy as we headed back to the village where the lieutenant and his people lived. Once we arrived, a conversation arose about what to do with the Italian Fascist prisoner. After some discussion between the two South African sergeant-majors and the *Patrioti*, they took the prisoner out to an open field. They stripped the man of his clothes, sent him running in a field, and shot him dead. That business—making him run—no doubt added a little sport to the whole thing.

I tried to get that picture out of my head. Unfortunately it was one of those ugly things that just keep coming back to you for a long time, like a graphic scene in a bad movie that plays over and over again in your head. It's so much harder when the reality of war is brought down to one single person. People were suffering and dying in great numbers, but the killing of this one guy, a Fascist who nevertheless, given the chance, might have killed us all, really got to me.

This war was teaching me something over and over again. From the day I entered the service, I had seen supposedly brutal people acting in a civilized manner and supposedly civilized people acting in a brutal manner. That's what war does, I guess. What had it done to me?

So the *Patrioti* and the South African sergeant-majors, these supposedly civilized men, fought to see who would get the man's boots. In fairness to them, every good soldier knows that good boots can save your life.

I didn't go out to the field to watch the execution. None of the British went. Even Captain Schuster stayed behind. But we heard about it, and it was a hard thing to shake free.

———

The always enterprising *Patrioti* stole another truck. Stealing trucks was something they apparently excelled in and thoroughly enjoyed. This time it was a big flatbed.

As we were saying our goodbyes to the lieutenant and the villagers, I noticed the two South Africans and Chuck in a heated discussion that was quickly escalating into a flat-out fight. As I approached them, one of the South Africans suddenly pulled out his pistol, pointed it at Chuck, and said, "Why, I ought to shoot you!"

"Wait a minute, wait a minute!" I said. "No one's going to shoot anyone. Now, what's the trouble?"

"This, this bloke here," the sergeant-major sputtered, "he's trying to get us to leave all of you fellows behind and take only 'im!"

Chuck made no response as he stormed away.

"Yep, he was trying to convince us we'd do better without youse and we should leave you on your own and only take the great Ranger."

"Look, no one is going to leave anyone behind," I said. "There's room for everyone."

We couldn't afford to turn against each other now. I wasn't all that shocked at Chuck. I always knew that he was out for himself alone. (That's why I'll never understand, nor forget, his waiting for me to recover from pneumonia.) But I wasn't surprised that he would try to pull something like that and I guess that's why I wasn't angry. He made no secret of the fact that he was out for himself. And for all of his negative qualities, I have to say that unlike a lot of other guys in our situation, Chuck did behave like a gentleman and only slipped up once.

Late one evening while we were eating, the Italian lieutenant came over to me and said, "Your captain is in the cantina. He has been drinking too much, I think. With the young women around, there could be trouble. You had better get him out of there."

Chuck and I had never discussed our feelings about booze and women and gambling and such. But I think he knew where I stood and he seemed to feel the same way I did: it was just too dangerous. As escapees behind enemy lines, we had enough to worry about. Sure, a lot of guys take advantage of being in a war to do things they wouldn't ordinarily do. Chuck and I had always rejected offers and opportunities that could have led us into that kind of misery. So even though I knew Chuck was very different from me in many ways, I felt sure there would be no real problem in the cantina.

When I went in and saw him, it was clear that what the lieutenant had told me was true. I walked over to Chuck and quietly suggested we leave. Without a word, he pulled himself together and walked out and we never spoke of it.

Schuster and I were at odds about a lot of things, no doubt about it. But I knew he had some good basic instincts. I didn't understand why he would want to leave anyone behind, but the matter was dropped and that's the way I wanted to leave it.

———

Once the South Africans had settled down and the decision had been made that we would all head for the coast again and try to link up with those British subs, we climbed into the truck. One of the sergeant-majors got into the driver's seat; the other sat beside him in the middle with a *Patrioto* next to the door. Ben and the other Brits, Schuster, and I crawled under a tarp and lay down on our bellies at the front end of the shallow truck bed nearest the cab. Last, four *Patrioti* got under the tarp near the opening in the back, with their guns ready. We were on our way.

After a while the truck stopped. We had apparently

come to a roadblock manned by several heavily armed *cara-biniere* loyal to the *Fascisti*. Through a crack I could see some guards standing beside a shed about thirty feet from our truck with machine guns aimed at us. One of the other men whispered that he could see another machine gunner on the opposite side of the road. We could hear one of the guards from the shed approach the passenger side of the truck. He told the *Patrioto* sitting next to the window that they would have to inspect the back of the truck. The *Patrioto*, who had been hiding a grenade on his lap, pulled the pin and dropped the thing out of the window. "Boom!" The grenade blasted the guard into eternity. Just as quickly, machine-gun fire coming from the direction of the shed brushed my shoulder and ripped through the sideboard of the truck body, tearing it to pieces. The sergeant-major at the wheel tried to gun the engine to get us the hell out of there. But the truck stalled. The *Patrioti* threw back the tarp and began firing. I watched as the guard by the shed fell at the very moment our truck engine jerked back to life. Off we went, careening down the twisted and muddy road, machine-gun fire chasing after us. Mercifully we were heading down a hill through a wooded area that protected us. The truck raced on, turning here and there for about fifteen minutes before pulling aside into a thicket so that we could regroup.

Situations change quickly in a war. Now that there had been bloodshed, we knew they'd be looking for us—all of us. There was no longer safety in numbers. In spite of what had happened with Chuck only hours earlier, Schuster, Bender, and I talked it over and decided that we would attract too much attention if we all stayed together. We told the *Patrioti* that the three of us would go off on our own.

"No, no," they protested, "stay with us. We'll get you to the subs. We can protect you. It's too dangerous on your own."

But the three of us held to our position. Even the South Africans reluctantly agreed with our plan. I don't know what the others intended to do, but to this day I pray that they weren't captured.

After an emotional farewell, we headed on foot toward the town of Macerata. It was still morning when we set off, and nearly evening when we first sighted Macerata. To reach the town, we had to walk through the outskirts of a small village and cross a stream. When I was in the middle of the small footbridge, I looked down into the swiftly flowing stream and began to tear apart the journal I had been keeping for some time. I watched the tiny pieces of it flow downstream toward where I wanted to be—the Adriatic Sea.

The killing at the roadblock had put us in danger. I had no choice but to destroy that journal, having recorded and sketched the incident in detail. Perhaps it is not surprising that I can remember so much of it now; the experience was intense enough to burn its way into my mind and heart. That day on the little bridge, even though I was certain I was doing the right thing, I did feel some regret about destroying my notes and sketches, because I'm a storyteller at heart. In the end I sacrificed my journal for the sake of self-preservation. I kept that journal in order to hang on to what was happening; I don't know if I intended it to be read by anyone else necessarily. But it was a dangerous thing and could have cost the lives of some of the people who saved ours.

We were fairly sure they would be hunting for the people who killed the guards, but we figured they would be looking for a gang that was trying to avoid the towns. Bender, Schuster, and I hoped that the three of us walking into a town wouldn't look as though we were on the run.

When we finally got into the town, people were reluctant to house all three of us. We were much closer to the front now and we understood the fear the people had. Anzio had fallen, Rome had been liberated, the Allies were pushing northward now, and the Germans were pulling back. All good news at last, but great danger at the same time. There were a lot of desperate people making a final stand. Once we found a friendly family, they would usually agree to house one of us and split the other two between other partisan homes. In the morning we'd meet up again and decide whether it was safe to head south or more prudent to sit tight a while longer. Now that the weather was warmer, we could sleep in sheds and barns when necessary. With the new season more Italians were outdoors, too. We'd pass hundreds of people, most of them women, working in the fields. In the villages and towns, you could tell the time of day by the number of people sitting on kitchen chairs out in front of their houses, enjoying a little gossip in the late-afternoon sun.

The Ranger Captain and the Sub

Some distance south of Macerata, we stopped for the night and were put up separately in houses a mile or so apart. Just after dawn Ben came to the house where I was staying. Looking fresh and rested, he suggested we head over right away to where Chuck was staying so that we could make some progress that day.

I always enjoyed Ben's company. He was even-tempered and full of bright conversation and often hilarious observations. One lovely spring evening Ben stepped out of a barn where we were staying only to be accosted by a horrible odor that seemed to have settled around us. Without missing a beat, he took a deep breath, turned to us and, using an exaggerated Queen's English, said, "I say, it appears the villagers here are celebrating their annual *gahbage* burning festival tonight."

I admired his good sense and typically British talent for making the best of things. The Brits had earned the respect of the world with their ability to withstand relentless pummeling and unspeakable devastation—and make it look easy. Ben's humor was a great relief to me from the cynical, brooding Schuster who seemed to live perpetually in a dark and quiet misery.

Now, years later, I have a better understanding of the horror that Schuster experienced in the war. I know how hard he tried at Anzio to keep things together long after all was lost. I know how hard he fought to avoid capture for himself and his men. I saw his face when he realized that the other building back at Cisterna had been bombed by our own, killing even more of his Rangers. I knew all of that about him then, but I understand it better now.

Ben had been through a lot, too. He had spent two years

in prison. He was captured in North Africa by Rommel's troops, and brought to an Italian prison camp near Bologna. He escaped after Italy capitulated. Hell, Ben had been gone from home so long that he had a four-year-old daughter he had never seen. Ben told me that he prayed every night that his family somehow knew he had been taken prisoner and was alive. He couldn't bear the thought of them mourning his death. I understood that.

I knew better than to compare one person's war experience against another's. I learned back in Basic that your actions depended upon what you brought with you into the service. Everything you did reflected the kind of person you were inside, the way you were raised, what your beliefs were. I knew how lucky I was to have been raised by Frank and Antonia Mauritz. I figured that my friend Ben had been brought up by good people, too.

Enjoying the lush, heavily scented air on this particular May morning, Ben and I passed chestnut and olive trees in bloom and made our way to the little house where Chuck had spent the night. We knew immediately when the farmer opened the door that something was wrong. He seemed surprised to see us and then he asked, *"Perche non sieti andati con il Capitano?"* ("Why didn't you go with the Captain?")

"Go?" I said. "Where did the Captain go?"

"He went with the men who came last night. *Due inglesi.*"

"Due inglesi?" Ben echoed. "Oh God, two Englishmen. Where there *inglesi* here last night?"

We listened carefully as the farmer explained in Italian, "From the submarines, you understand? They came to take him. It was still early in the evening, only a little after dark. Understand? I don't really know anything, just that he left with them."

As the truth took form like a solitary figure emerging out of the fog, I heard Ben say quietly and without anger, "So he's gone on and left us, has he?" and then, almost as an afterthought, "Signore, did you hear him say anything to them about us?"

"No. *Niente.*" Nothing.

I don't remember much more of that conversation except that the farmer was afraid that we might hold him responsible. We did our best to assure him that we didn't. But mostly I just have an image of the two of us turning away from the house to head south on foot. I don't think Ben and I even spoke much as we took those first few steps away from the house. We were lost in our own thoughts, I guess. The subs had been our great hope for so long. Sometimes they took on a mythical, elusive quality, but always they held out hope. Now one of them had actually come, just as we had been told they would. But Chuck had done the unthinkable. Sure, he had given me reason to doubt him, especially when he tried to get the two South Africans to take him alone and leave us behind. Now he had actually done it.

By escaping with me, Chuck had abandoned his comrades behind lines. I'd like to think that's why he was so anxious to get back to fighting again: to come to their aid. The truth is, he had shown me from the beginning that he was a loner, and he had never pretended to be anything else. He was like a cat, keeping to himself, looking out for himself. What difference would it have made to him to tell the British commandos about Ben and me? That was the hardest thing to understand. The commandos were looking to pick up as many as possible. What possible difference would it have made to pick up two more?

As those first hours passed, I relived many of the odd things Chuck had done and said during our months together. His betrayal of us deepened the mystery that surrounded him while simultaneously exposing the true nature of the man. Sadly, I don't believe Chuck ever in his life felt that essential solidarity, that connection with other human beings. Maybe he did have that with his men, his Rangers. He had risked his life in battle many times. But that feeling of solidarity didn't extend to other people. Oh, I guess I'll never fully grasp it.

Amazingly, in this war, this long and terrible war, that

solidarity showed itself often and in many unexpected places. It was the light in the darkness. People risking all for others, perfect strangers, not because they were going to get anything back, not even because they were on the same side. No, there were acts of bravery and kindness performed only because we are fellow humans making our way in this world. To many, that connection is stronger than any politics or ideology. Chuck seemed to want no part of that. That's the way he was.

All of this went round and round in my head, but at last I came to the realization that Chuck would have to remain a mystery. I couldn't afford anger or even disappointment now. I looked at Ben who had suffered the same blow and was taking it like the gentle man he was. I resolved not to expend myself on Chuck Schuster but to keep going, just as I had been doing since that long-ago morning in January when I crashed *Skipper* into Anzio Bay.

The Long Walk Back

Ben and I fell into the usual routine of walking the back roads, staying inland for safety and, despite getting closer to the front, still finding kind, generous and brave people who were willing to give us food and shelter. One family who lived not far from a river near the town of Corridonia, I believe, invited us in for a meal of young spring greens fried with eggs.

Now that spring had come to Italy, there was an explosion of life: fruits, flowers, early vegetables, and greens covered the landscape and the tables. The countryside was dressed in delicate colors as trees burst into new leaf and the fields, hillsides, and vineyards came alive under the magnificence of the Italian sun. I will never forget the variety of ways we were served those new greens—*verdura,* they call them. We'd have them with white beans in a thick soup, tossed with vinegar and olive oil as a salad, fried in garlic and olive oil or, as was the case this day, served up in an omelet.

Ben and I were enjoying the aroma of the housewife's fresh baked bread and looking forward to her wonderful *frittata* when her husband rushed inside, yelling, "The priests are coming! Hurry, hide!"

We had become accustomed to fast exits and we asked no questions as we jumped to our feet and followed our host into the bedroom. We had just enough time to slip behind the open door when we heard the wife greeting her visitors. We held our breath as we listened to her and her husband exchange pleasantries with the priests. Then we became aware that the priests were moving around the house chanting something in a ceremonial way. It was Latin! "Oh Lord," I thought, "they're blessing the house!" Sure enough, they were coming closer. Now they were at the bedroom door, just inches from us. After a few seconds that seemed like an hour, they moved on without actually entering the room. Instead, they only tossed a few drops of holy water into it, accompanied by a blessing, before returning to the kitchen where our host expressed his gratitude. They all sat down for a glass of wine. I even heard the wife inviting the priests to join them for their mid-day meal.

"Oh no!" I thought. "Not our wonderful fried greens with eggs and fresh bread!" Thankfully, the priests declined, saying they had just eaten at the house down the road. There was a little talk about the war and some gossip and then, praise the Lord, they were gone.

"It's safe now," our host called out to us. When we were seated again at the table, the wife said, "Please don't misunderstand about the priests."

"What she means is," her husband interrupted, "we didn't make you hide because we know for sure the priests are *Fascisti*. The truth is, we don't know. And what if someone started asking questions or got them to talk? You know what I mean? This was the best thing."

We assured them we understood and continued enjoying our beautiful lunch.

———

It was late in June, and Ben and I were now very close to the front. We were staying together in a house, sharing a little side room off the family's main room. For the safety of the family, Ben and I spent our days out in a field hiding in a ditch. We were stalled there, because the Germans were swarming the area just south of us. That ditch was a good hiding place, and it was there that we met two Scots who were also escapees trying to get through the lines.

By this time there were a lot of young fighting men who had been away from home for a very long time. Even the barest glimpse of family life as we had once known it could trigger a yearning that could just tear you apart. Sometimes you saw a mother with her children, or a housewife hanging clothes out to dry. The hominess of these images stirred your deepest desires to get back home, to see your mom, hug your girl, fix your car, kiss your babies, whatever it was you were missing most. From our hiding place in that ditch, we could watch the daily life of an Italian family with a bunch of nice kids who played out in the yard. One of the Scottish fellows developed such a fondness for the family that he began sneaking up to the house to visit with them each day. We'd chuckle as we'd hear him whooping and playing with the children. After a time he would slip back to the safety of the ditch. On one occasion when the young man had been gone a little longer than usual, his companion became worried and slipped up to the house to see what was keeping him. When he returned, he was shaking his head. The distraught mother had told him that the Germans had come to the house before the young Scottish soldier could get away, and he had been recaptured.

The Front

It was strange to finally get close to the front. One day we were behind German artillery pointing toward the British who were just up ahead. The next day we noticed that the Germans had moved their artillery back a little to the north side of the River Tronto, I think it was. Ben and I were on the south side of the river, and it was then that we realized we were going through the front. There was a road up ahead that came to a Y. On one side of the road was a cornfield with all of the stalks from the year before, dried and cut down to a few inches. As we approached, we heard the whine of a shell and saw the explosion just up ahead in the cornfield. Bender, who was an artillery captain, explained to me that the Germans were using the field for artillery practice.

Seeing that I was ready to get the hell away from that field, Ben said, "Wait now, chap. They're likely not firing at us. This is practice. You'll see, the next one will be short. They've fired their long one and next will come a short one and then they'll know just how to hit smartly right in the middle."

Although his words did nothing to relieve my fear of being blown apart, I was interested as he went on to explain how they made a chart when the battle began so that they wouldn't have to sight in to hit a mark. They simply referred to the coordinates they had charted during practice. Sure enough, Bender was right, all too right, because the next one, the short one, exploded not fifty feet from us. When we hit the ground, I cut my hand on the stump of a corn stalk and marveled, as usual, at Bender's classic cool.

"Just so, Mauritz, that was the short one," he announced, more pleased with being right than with being missed by the blast.

To me, this was the one that nearly got us. But it turned out that Captain Bender was right again: there were no more explosions while we were in that neighborhood.

Things now happened quickly. Off in the distance, far beyond the cornfield, we saw, of all things, a big, thick-bodied American MP. We had made it! Just as easy as that, we approached him. I pulled my dog tags out and unbuttoned my shirt so that my flight suit could be seen, and began explaining, "Me and the Captain here just came through the front. We were in prisons up north. I escaped five months ago. Mauritz is my name and this is Captain...." And that was it. I told my story, Ben told his, and we were back. Another MP was called over. It was all very simple. We were taken to field headquarters. On the way we saw some Free Polish troops with a group of German prisoners. One of the prisoners, a private, called out to me. I recognized him from two weeks earlier.

"Hey, Yank!" he said in German. "Tell them, please, I deserted way back there. I was with the Italians. I'm not the enemy. Tell them. I was finished with this damn war a long time ago."

I did tell them. He had been living with the Italians. He was one of those who simply quit the war. Toward the end, as the Allies began their successful push northward, I saw a lot of German deserters who were "captured" by the Italians. It was just the way the war was winding down in Italy. That brief conversation with the German soldier was the last time I used my German in the war. In fact, it was in many ways the last of the war for me.

There was a funny moment before we were moved out of this area just south of Pescara. A lot of British were in the area and some men from their navy spotted Ben. These British naval officers were assigned to a submarine that was just offshore. When we told them how long we had been hoping to be picked up by a British sub, one of them replied, "Well, consider yourselves picked up now. We're inviting you to dine with us

187

on our sub," adding, with a wink to me, "so this Yank here can't say the Brits are floating around with their heads up their arses, seeing as how we missed picking you up and all."

With that we were shuttled to a dinghy and rowed out to the sub. I'll never forget the wild rocking of that dinghy out there in the Adriatic nor my amazement as we bobbed up to that big slap of a sub that lay in the water as still as a tombstone. That night we ate and drank with gusto, toasting everyone and everything in sight. I can't tell you how the conversation got around to it, but somehow Ben and I learned that we were on the very sub that had rescued Chuck. Maybe it was the drink or maybe it was my brain not wanting to hold onto that bit of information, but the next day I checked with Ben to be certain that I hadn't imagined anything. He confirmed that we had indeed dined on the very sub we had missed while we were back there behind the lines.

When the time came for Ben and me to say goodbye, it happened too quickly to be able to think or say much. We each knew how the other felt. Our friendship had grown naturally out of humor and shared interests and sensibilities. Looking back with what I hope is a deepened maturity and perhaps even a little more wisdom, I am grateful that Ben came into my life when he did. His presence eased much of the tension and uncertainty I felt with Chuck. Through his simplicity and grace under pressure, Ben taught me a lot by his example. He was the quintessential gentleman officer, possessing the great strength to hold fast to his civility, his ethics, and his reason in the face of cruelty, brutality, and chaos.

"This is it then, Mauritz."

"The very best of luck to you, Ben," I think I said, extending my hand. "You'll be seeing that little kid of yours soon now."

"Straight away! You take care. It's been grand knowing you." He patted me on the arm. Someone called out. There was a quick sort of hug, I remember, then Ben turned to leave. He

188

took a few long strides to catch up with the others before look-ing back over his shoulder and shouting to me, "Keep up with your bridge game, you're not half bad."

"I will," I shouted back. "It was grand knowing you too, Ben." And he was gone.

The End of the Story

On a sweltering June 25 I was debriefed at Air Force Headquarters in Foggia. When I was asked to give the details of my escape and evasion (I was officially tagged an escapee since I had not been held long enough to be called a prisoner of war), I explained how Captain Schuster and I had slipped out of the prison camp at Laterina and walked across the mountains.

At my first mention of Chuck's name, my examiner said, "Yes, Captain Charles Schuster, a Ranger. He came through here about a month ago. Picked up by a sub as I recall. He didn't mention you." After a pause, he added, "I guess he did a lot of damage back there behind lines."

I could have said a lot of things at that moment, but what would be the good? So I simply said, "No damage that I saw, sir," and was done with it. With those words I put an end to this thing with Chuck. They set me free of him in some way.

—

My examiner, seeing a bandage on my hand, asked if I had been wounded in any way behind the lines.

"No," I said, "this is just a cut I got when I fell in a cornfield."

"Were you behind the lines at the time? Did you require medical attention?"

"Well, yes. I mean, we didn't know where the lines were at the time."

"Well then, we'll put you down for a Purple Heart, because you were wounded behind enemy lines. That is considered a battle wound, and if you were treated by a doctor—"

"No, no!" I told him, almost laughing. "The Purple Heart means too much. I could never accept that for this little cut. And I really don't know where the line was then. No

190

absolutely, no thanks," I said.

A Purple Heart! I had not been wounded. My mind swept back over the whole landscape of my experience: the crash landing in the bay at Anzio, my capture, the march through Rome, the escape, the long walk across Italy's boot. Wounded? Not in any way. If anything, I would say I had been gifted, blessed. (Even during the very worst of it: when we were shot at, or when Schuster abandoned us. All those months of tension and fear, all of it was a life experience, deep and true.) The kind of thing that makes you stronger and hopefully a lot wiser. And, I mean to say, that was the worst of it. Even the blackest times were rich with learning. But at best I had been given a glimpse into human nature that revealed most of my fellow beings as kind and generous, caring and brave. How had I gotten so lucky? Here I was in the middle of what surely will be remembered as one of mankind's most terrible experiences. Yet, here I was feeling as if I had been given a wonderful gift, this ability to see people at their very best during the very worst.... Oh, so that's what my old English teacher in high school was trying to teach us when we read *A Tale of Two Cities.* She was trying to get us to understand what Charles Dickens meant by his opening line, "It was the best of times, it was the worst of times." How could I have known I would live that to the fullest? But my "worst" did not wound me in any way. I deserved no medals for my experience. I had already been given a great reward. I knew it then, but what I couldn't have guessed on that summer day of my debriefing was how this experience of mine would continue to open to me far into the future, long after I thought I had put it away.

Home

The moment I signed the document swearing that I would talk to no one about my experiences behind lines, I was told that I had to be out of the theater of operation within seven days. I barely had time for a shower and a good night's sleep before I was shipped back to North Africa, where I was put on a plane for New York. Everything happened so fast that I have few memories of those hectic days. The details of this time don't come into focus for me until I boarded the plane for the States. I was seated next to a young army officer named Bill. We were both excited about going home and seeing our families again. Hearing that my parents would be notified made me realize that I had been carrying around a terrible guilt over the pain I had caused them. I had prayed that they hadn't given up hope that I was alive; I had willed them to know that I was still in this world. Now they would be certain. As for me, something that had felt like a cold, hard stone in my stomach began to disappear. These thoughts brought Ben to mind. Was he back in England, seeing his child for the first time? I hoped so.

I know now that I suffered a kind of confusion during those last days overseas. With everything happening so quickly, I had trouble processing the fact that a chapter of my life—one that had been so deeply etched—had closed abruptly. Decades later I would sympathize with the Vietnam veterans who were whisked from those hellish jungles and deposited back in the States too quickly. I understood. And though all war is terrible, I don't believe the campaign in Italy came close to the horrors of Southeast Asia. That was a very different war.

I had been sent from Italy swiftly, but Italy was slow in leaving me. No one could have known from my actions or talk that my mind was running a continuous movie of places, faces, voices, and sounds of the life that had been mine for the past five months. All that was Italy seemed more real to me than what was happening around me now.

Bill and I knew we would be staying in New York for a few days until we could get transportation to our hometowns. During the flight we made plans for a big time in the big city. Although I know we talked about our war experiences, I don't remember the circumstances under which Bill was returning home. He was most likely just as confused and disoriented as I. We didn't really open up to each other on that flight home even though there we were, two young bucks coming home in one piece with a city like New York waiting. But I suppose that in those days, in that war, reflection and soul-baring would have been unthinkable.

I had never been to New York. When our plane made its descent over Manhattan, the sight of the sprawling landscape below us had a strange effect on me. The towering buildings and the traffic scurrying like insects unleashed a jumble of images that transfixed me: planes, prisoners, guards, frozen creeks, rushing water. Water coming closer and closer. *Skipper*. *Skipper* landing. Trying to keep its nose above water. And, finally, *Skipper* disappearing into the sea...

————

"The Waldorf-Astoria! Mike, we're staying at the Waldorf! You ever heard of it?"

"Sure. You think I'm some Pittsburgh hayseed?"

"Want to get a cab? I've always wanted to ride in one."

I did my best to be enthusiastic, but my head whirled with the swarm of traffic and people. I felt tired and desolate.

We slept for hours in the grand old Waldorf-Astoria and, after long showers, we were ready for New York City. I had slept off and scrubbed away much of the muddle that had made my return home a tough transition. I felt excited now about being back in the States. We were ready to hit the streets. Bill and I popped into every bar we saw, relishing the good whiskey and beautiful girls—not that they weren't beautiful in Italy, but in the States I felt more at ease enjoying the view. There was music everywhere, live bands, jukeboxes, radios. I had never heard so much music. Some girls asked us to dance in one of the places. I'm not much of a dancer but, on that night, I danced a lot.

We celebrated our return in a big way during those two days in New York City. Then we said our goodbyes and boarded our separate trains with massive hangovers and very little cash in our pockets.

I slept during most of the ride home. It was late, after midnight, when the train pulled into the Turtle Creek station. My parents had no telephone. I couldn't be sure that they had been notified of my return yet. But it was balmy and I savored the quiet walk up the hill home. Home. I was walking home. I was walking home from the war without a scratch. God had been so good to me.

On the way, I was conscious of the smells—the grass, the roses growing up trellises on the sides of porches, the distant mills and smokestacks. Home. All was quiet and strange, and yet as familiar as my own hand. My senses had confronted so many different things—the expanse of sky and desert in North Africa, the sea and the mountains; the roar of plane engines, the thunderous impact of bombs; the smell of gasoline and of burning; the aroma of salt air and mountain air. Yes, this warm summer night in a mill town in Pennsylvania surrounded me like a blanket with the feel of home. Everything was still here, intact, as if it had been suspended during my absence. Everything frozen and waiting for me. Even blindfolded I would have known where I was.

The moon lit my way as I walked up our hill past all the houses, each sitting a little higher than the one before. This was the same moon I had watched high in the Apennines, the one I hoped to hitch a ride on to take me home. Over there, the moon had given me a strange feeling, especially when I was a prison-

194

er. There we all were, no longer free, unsure of our fate. And above us was the very moon that had shone down on our backyards at home and would do so again in a few hours. It seemed to me now that the moon had followed me home.

As I continued heading home, I thought about the times I saw my birth mother walking up the hill, carrying groceries to the Susco house a few blocks above ours. As a teenager I gave her a ride home now and then, even though it was a rash thing to do. My parents would have been hurt and angry if they had known that I had associated with her—especially my mother, who harbored a fear that my birth family would somehow win me over. But I hadn't been caught, and there was no danger of my biological mother ever replacing my adopted mother. Antonia Mauritz was Mother to me in every sense of the word. Helen Susco was blood, but blood only. Even though I once sent her my sketch of a pretty girl I had met—a girl who would ultimately become my wife, Helen Susco would forever remain in the shadows of my life.

Now I was coming home to Antonia, my mother. As our house came into view, my heart beat faster. I bounded up the wooden porch steps as I had always done. I knocked on the door and through the open windows I heard my father call, "Who is it?"

"It's me! Mickey! I'm home!"

From inside came, "Oh my Gott, oh my Gott!"

Just two days earlier my parents had been notified that I had returned from behind enemy lines, that I was alive. Our reunion was awash in emotion. My father rushed forward with a handshake, then a crushing hug, while patting me on the back and losing his struggle to hold back tears that I had never seen before. My mother, too overcome to speak, held me tightly and sobbed. She felt like a fragile, shaking bird. At last she looked at me, touched my face, and managed, "My boy. Tank Gott."

Later, sitting at the kitchen table, I could only answer their flood of questions with the thinnest of details. In those early morning hours I was too spent to begin telling them of my adventures. All I needed or wanted at that moment was to look at their faces and to absorb the fact that I was home. In the gray morning hours of my homecoming day, when we finally said good night, I was overwhelmed by the pure, simple comfort of our house and my bed. My bed. "I'm home," I remember thinking, "in my bed, with Mom and Pop just down the hall."

The truth is that even after I adjusted to being home, I was content to keep my memories of Italy locked in storage. The story had ended well. I had done the best I could. Now I was ready to move on.

The Letter

January, 1998

I was retired from U. S. Steel's Edgar Thompson Works in Braddock, Pennsylvania. Louise and I had built a close and loving marriage. We were content. Our two children, Donna and Craig, were grown and busy with their families and careers. We had four wonderful grandchildren, and though I was in my late seventies, I was blessed with good health and energy.

Louise and I still lived in the house where we had raised our children. Our neighborhood had changed a lot, but we planned to stay in our house as long as God gave us the strength to take care of it.

After my parents and the Suscos passed on, I did get to know my biological brothers and sisters a little better. Over the years, we developed a warm friendship for which I have been grateful.

The day I want to tell you about was mild for Pennsylvania in January. On this particular afternoon I returned home from a round of errands—post office, gas station, hardware store. It was an ordinary day, as far as I could tell. It didn't feel any different to me. My sensors, which used to be pretty good, must have been lulled by the seamlessness of our lives since my retirement. There were no hints at all that it would become one of those markers in the map of your life, the moment when you would begin to ask yourself, "Now, did that happen before or after?"

As I entered the house that day, everything changed. "I'm back," I called to Louise.

From the living room she answered, "You better come look at this letter, Mickey." She showed me an envelope with foreign stamps addressed to Michael Mauritz. Then I saw the return address: it was from Italy. A tiny bell went off somewhere in my head as I tore open the envelope and read:

Dear Mr. Mauritz,

First of all, let me ask you to forgive me if I'm disturbing you without even knowing if you are the person I'm trying to contact!

I had two first impressions and both turned out to be correct. I knew instantly that I was the Mauritz he was looking for. Second, the tentative and respectful beginning touched me. I knew the letter had been written by a kind and gentle person. The writer continued in English that was clearly a second language:

After this strange beginning, let me introduce myself: I am an Italian aviation historian and from over twenty years I have been working on the study of the aerial operations that took place in Italy from 1943 to 1945. I've also published several books both in the U. S. and in England....

It occurred to me that he might be writing to tell me about a reunion. I never could have anticipated what came next:

What brought me to write this letter to you, however, was caused by an event that took place a few weeks ago and which I was involved into: the rescue of a Curtiss P-40 fighter from the sea near Anzio.

Rescue? Is this what he was writing about? I had seen my plane go down! And too much time has passed.

A few weeks ago I was contacted by a search divers team to identify the submerged plane on the basis of the data

*found on the fuselage.... The P-40L Serial Number 42-10857
belonged to 79th FG, 86th FS, Coded X4 and bore the nickname*
Skipper *on port side....*

It *was Skipper*! *Skipper* had been found!

*It was the personal mount of Lieutenant E. E. Parsons
(his name being painted ahead of the cockpit). On January 31,
1944, however, it wasn't flown by him.*

That's right, because it was flown by me! The writer
knew that too, from an official report which identified me as the
pilot. The report confirmed that I had been on a reconnaissance
mission over the Anzio beachhead and speculated that I had
been hit by ground fire. I was sure that I hadn't been hit, but I
also had never been able to figure out what caused the plane's
engine to overheat.   The next part of the letter was eerie:

*Last time he was seen he had reached the shore and
was trying to hide in a bush with German troops heading
towards him. He was listed as Missing in Action (presumably
Prisoner of War).*

It was like reading my own obituary. But I had little time
to take that in, because the writer then announced that *Skipper*
had been brought ashore "virtually intact and in really remarkable condition." The story of *Skipper*'s recovery had been featured on the Sunday-evening television news in Italy.

All this time I had been reading the letter aloud so that
Louise could hear it too. She hadn't said a word, but now I
looked up at her and saw the puzzled look on her face. She and
the kids knew my war history, but they didn't know it in detail.
Once I was back in the states, I was assigned to train gunners
to fire on fighter planes.   They used cameras on their guns in
place of ammunition to record the accuracy of their shooting.

I found it to be fascinating and important work. But the truth was that in those days, I spent little time thinking about my experiences in Italy. When the war ended, I went back to work and my life just went on from there. I had lived what anyone would call a happy, productive, fulfilled life. My marriage was rock-solid and I had a good relationship with my children. I was a typical post-war father who delighted in seeing his children grow up in an era of peace and plenty, television, hula hoops, rock 'n' roll. It was a good time to be a kid and an even better time to be a parent.

I was an active union member. I kept an interested eye on politics. Most importantly, through my wife and daughter I found myself on a pathway of learning and growth that led me to rebirth in the Lord Jesus Christ.

———

After my adoptive and birth parents passed away and I became closer to my siblings, I learned more facts about my birth and adoption. This knowledge did nothing to alter the deep affection I had for Frank and Antonia Mauritz, but I enjoyed getting to know my brothers and sisters. There was one incident, however, that disturbed me.

While I was at Capodichino, I ran into my birth sister's husband who was also stationed there. After the war when I was becoming acquainted with the Susco family, I learned that my sister's husband knew I had been forced down at Anzio and that he had enough information to conclude I had been captured alive. He relayed this news in a letter to his wife who in turn informed my birth parents. Sadly, because of the ugly feud between the Suscos and my adoptive family, the information was never shared with Frank and Antonio Mauritz. The Mauritzes knew only that I was missing in action. It hurt me to think of the anguish my parents suffered those months between my crash landing in January and my return home in June. I know they held out little hope for my survival. How could they when my name was posted among the war dead on a document at the Westinghouse plant!

Soon after my homecoming my father, overcome with relief and gratitude, escorted me down to the plant to see my name in the window. That posting of my name apparently evoked a response from someone else, too. It seems that a beautiful young woman, whom I had met briefly before being shipped out, had taken notice of my name on the list of war dead. The young woman, who had only recently moved to Turtle Creek from West Virginia, had taken a job at the local five-and-ten-cent store. It was on a lovely summer day that she glanced out of the store's big plate-glass window and, upon seeing this tall thin fellow loping across the street, exclaimed to her fellow clerks, "Oh Lord, there goes a dead man!"

Of course, that "dead man" was me, and it wasn't long before the pretty young clerk and I were an item about town. Soon, we became husband and wife.

———

So here we were, Louise and I, on this day in January, 1998 (dear Lord, it was almost fifty-four years to the day that I ditched my plane!), absorbing the news that was casting us back into the war years as nothing had succeeded in doing before.

I don't know if the real Michael Mauritz is still alive and if he survived to the capture and the imprisonment. What I do know, however, is that I had to try to locate him or some of his relatives in the U. S.

The writer told me of his online search through the white pages and his discovery of only five Michael Mauritzes. "Only five," he said. My reaction was, "My goodness, there are five of us!"

I read to Louise that these fellows—these divers and this historian fellow—would like me or someone from my family to attend a ceremony in Italy for the public unveiling of *Skipper*.

I hope that you could help me to bring back together the man and the machine and, while thanking you for your kind attention and patience in reading me so far, I wait for your welcome reply and remain…

The letter was signed Ferdinando d'Amico. *Amico* is the Italian word for friend.

And so it began.

"A ceremony?" Louise asked. "What kind of ceremony would they have for a plane? I don't understand."

"I'm as much in the dark about this as you are," I told her. "But I assume we'll be hearing more about all of this. In the meantime, I guess I'd better write back and own up to being that fellow who ditched his plane in the bay fifty-four years ago."

In truth, I wasn't at all in the dark. It was incredible that *Skipper* had been found after more than half a century under the sea. But the opportunity to attend the ceremony would never have arisen had it not been for the kindness of the many Italians, mostly peasants, who had risked their lives to help me so long ago. It was the story of *Skipper*'s rescue that would bring my story to light. None of this would be happening if that plane hadn't been brought up out of the sea. What made them do it? I reread the letter. Signore d'Amico didn't explain.

From the day the letter arrived, my family bombarded me with questions. Their interest and enthusiasm was boundless, and I confess that I was thoroughly enjoying my journey back in time.

In my response to Signore d'Amico, I wrote:

You cannot imagine the surprise and welcome that my wife and I received with your letter dated January 20, 1998. I indeed am the person you are looking for.

On January 31, 1944, I was a second lieutenant stationed at Capodichino Airdrome in Naples. I was assigned to the 79th FG, 86th FS.

I was captured by three German soldiers before landing craft could reach me while I was hiding in the bushes along the shore.

I was taken behind lines on a motorcycle by two Germans and marched through Rome with other captured troops, and eventually was taken to a small town near Arezzo where we were placed in an unoccupied prison camp.

On February 9, 1944, Captain Charles Schuster (an American Ranger) and I escaped from that prison camp at about 11:00 a.m.

As we made our way to the Allied lines over the next five months, we were helped by many kind and generous Italian families. We crossed the Apennines Mountains and eventually made it to Ancona. Then we walked south and on June 25, 1944, I crossed the Allied lines and returned to Air Force headquarters based in Foggia. Best regards.

Sincerely,

Michael Mauritz

P. S. I have included copies from my logbook, an invoice for my train ride to Foggia, and a statement I had to sign concerning my escape and return behind Allied lines. I hope this information will be helpful. Last but not least, enclosed is a picture of my wife and myself taken in 1945. We are a little older now, but still very much in love. I am looking forward to telling you about my adventure. Please do not hesitate to contact me.

Letters, phone calls, and emails (my son, Craig, was able to receive) began flying back and forth. Eventually Craig steered me into the new cyberworld and I have been enjoying this miracle of communication on my own ever since.

Fallwell of Oklahoma

That letter from Signore d'Amico brought a lot of interesting people into my life. Hands down, the most memorable and colorful was the self-styled Oklahoma patriot Boyd Fallwell. Fallwell's Honor Guard Web site had understandably attracted the attention of the Italian colonel Euro Rossi who had led the dive for *Skipper*. Colonel Rossi and two of his lieutenants had been browsing on the Internet one day in hopes of finding *Skipper*'s pilot when they happened upon Fallwell's colorful site. When they contacted Fallwell and told him about *Skipper* and their efforts to find me, Fallwell sprang into action, sniffing about in the cyberworld like a hound dog on the scent of a rabbit, until he located me.

Unlike the gentle and respectful Ferdinando d'Amico who had written to me weeks earlier, Boyd Fallwell burst into my life over the phone wires like a sheriff in an old western pushing through the saloon doors. "Michael Mauritz?"

"That's me," I said. "What can I do for you?"

"Name's Boyd Fallwell. You the fighter pilot who put his plane down in the bay of Anzio during the war?"

"Me again," I said.

"Well, there's some Italian brass lookin' fer ya on the Internet and they come upon my Web site, 'Honor Guard.' Ever hear of it?"

"No, but—"

"They asked for my help and I found five Michael Mauritzes here in the States and you're the first one I called. Hot dog, I found you! First one! Well, anyway…"

And on he went about a Colonel Euro Rossi and the other divers and about how *Skipper* had been recovered intact from Anzio Bay and was now housed in the Piana delle Orme Museum.

Fallwell did his homework and knew his way through the maze of official military documents. As time went by, he shared the fruits of his research and had much more to tell me about my adventures than I ever dreamed were on record.

I was especially interested in the copy of a letter Boyd sent to me that he had received from U. S. Air Force archivist Lynn Gamma. She wrote: "Thank you for your emails. Attached is the Missing Air Crew report. It is quite interesting and makes you wonder about the rest of the story—how did Lieutenant Mauritz return to safety?"

Included in this report was the statement of Major Nielsen who was the formation leader the day that I ditched my plane. It was Major Nielsen to whom I radioed the message that my engine was overheating. He reported the event this way: "On 31st January, 1944, Lieutenant Mauritz made an emergency landing in the water near beach at G-068 110 after reporting his coolant temperature to be 150 degrees c. In response to a radio call to forward fighter control, a rescue launch arrived at the beach just as low gasoline compelled covering aircraft, one of which was flown by the undersigned, to leave the area."

This bit of information meant that while I was marched at gunpoint away from the beach after my capture, feeling desolate as the plane (probably Nielsen) circled and disappeared from view, the rescue launch had already arrived for me! Now another piece of the puzzle was in place. I read this, though, without any sense of regret that I missed the launch. I had long ago come to accept that my capture and escape had been my destiny. Nielsen's report went on to describe what he had seen before leaving the area: "Meantime Lieutenant Mauritz had got out of his airplane which was almost completely submerged, had waded to the beach, and took cover in the nearby bushes. I saw a man wearing a helmet moving cautiously through the bushes near where Lieutenant Mauritz had hidden."

I was fascinated with the thought that Nielsen saw *Skipper* disappearing into the sea and spotted the young

German soldier who captured me. It was probably this report, or word of it, that led my birth sister's husband to write home that I had been captured alive. I was beginning to realize how uniquely blessed I was. This story of mine, with its missing pieces so long ago buried in the bay, had surfaced and was being put together before my eyes. It was like a filmstrip of something once shattered being run backward in slow motion and showing all the fragments coming together as a whole again.

Fallwell's research uncovered another report, from a Captain Ewing who was also flying over the bay just after eleven o'clock on the morning I went down. It seems that this fellow and his flight officer saw a launch, probably the one that Nielsen had dispatched. Ewing reported that two men from the launch conducted a lengthy search of the beach, even walking inland all the way across the road nearest the shore. By this time I was probably on my way to that first house where they gave me a blanket. Ewing saw that the two men came up empty-handed, so he radioed them and learned that they had found my life jacket and an uninflated dinghy but no signs of blood or anything to indicate that I had been killed. Then, apparently, the Germans spotted the guys from the launch and started firing on them and they got out of there.

Fallwell put the story of *Skipper* and me up on his Web site, which he had set up to memorialize veterans. He asked for pictures of me when I was in the service as well as current pictures of me and Louise. He posted pictures of the dive and recovery of *Skipper* and found a permanent place in Louise's heart when he told us of his "Honor Guard of One" mission to see that as many vets as possible are laid to rest with military honors.

Louise loved hearing Boyd's story of his rebirth in Jesus as he languished for weeks in and out of veterans hospitals following his near-fatal heart attack. We agreed that maybe his heart had been broken in order to let in the great light and love of Christ which he now lavished on everyone he met. Boyd won our friendship with his warm and twangy cowboy humor and drawl, but he earned Louise's respect with his deep conviction that he must serve the Lord by honoring veterans. To this day she faithfully sends the big-hearted Oklahoma plumber-turned- minister twenty-five dollars a month to help him carry on his life's work.

I have to mention a few words here about my son, Craig, and my daughter, Donna. When they were growing up, they knew that I had to ditch my plane in Anzio Bay and they were even aware that I had been captured and ultimately escaped. I can't say how many details I added over the years, but it wasn't much. There was no reason for me to talk about it. I think their perception of my adventure in the war was that it was only mildly interesting, if that. Compared to many, my story was not one of fierce combat, daring, or suffering.

But the rescue of my plane from the sea, just where I told them I had ditched it, sparked a keen interest. As letters and phone calls began to come from all over the place, Craig and Donna's response to my story grew from casual interest to amazement to an almost insatiable appetite for details. They had no words when they saw the photos on Fallwell's Web site of the diving team bringing *Skipper* to the surface. They were stunned by the massive crowd scrambling over the dunes, ignoring government restrictions, to get a look at *Skipper*. Now they wanted to hear more about the crash, the capture, and the escape, but for the first time they wanted me to tell them about our long walk over the Apennines and the wonderful people who helped us.

Craig was so excited about my story and the recovery of *Skipper* that he notified our local paper. The write-up featured my old Air Force picture showing a smiling, smooth-faced young fellow who bore only a slight resemblance to the white-haired guy wearing glasses...except perhaps for the smile. To my great surprise, I was enjoying every bit of the attention and I found that I loved telling the story of *Skipper* and me and Italy.

From that feature-story came another flurry of calls and

people approaching me at church and about town, wanting to know more. Soon the two Pittsburgh papers picked up the story of *Skipper*'s recovery and ran the photos of Michael Mauritz (young and old). The crusted-over P-40L fighter plane was becoming well known.

The Ranger's Story

Reviving the past has an unsettling side to it. Louise was understandably apprehensive about the return of *Skipper*. She told me later, "I had mixed feelings about what it would mean for us." Referring to that first letter from Signore d'Amico, she said, "I really wanted to throw it in the trash, for fear it would disrupt our lives. We were very content."

I understood her fear, but I knew I would never let the past disrupt the peace of the present. Nothing and no one could ever change the fact that my marriage and family were the world to me. Still, the knowledge that I had had a very special war experience was buried deep inside me. The desire to share my story was growing stronger as I grew older. But life has a way of getting in front of such ideas, so my dream kept getting shoved to the back. Finally I just let it be, that is, until I read Signore d'Amico's letter. Dear God, the sea itself had released *Skipper*, resurrecting it from its grave to snag at some fishing nets and make its presence known. Now the Italians were claiming her as an historic relic, *their* relic. And they were honoring me by inviting *Skipper*'s pilot to be a part of all of this. The appeal was irresistible.

As time passed, Louise warmed to the idea of *Skipper*'s recovery and to our lives being illuminated a little by the "spotlight." After all, this wasn't just my story alone. Many people in Italy had gone to great lengths to recover the craft. I had learned that *Skipper* was the only intact P-40L in existence. And now this Signore de Pasquale was making *Skipper* the centerpiece of Piana delle Orme, his war museum near Anzio. In addition, many aviation historians from around the world were joining Ferdinando d'Amico in regarding *Skipper* as a great opportunity to further the study of aviation history.

I could never have imagined the number of people who, for many different reasons, had an interest in *Skipper*'s story. Shortly after the article ran in the *Pittsburgh Post Gazette*, I received a call from a fellow who introduced himself as Corporal Larry Schenkel of the U.S. Rangers. "You the Michael Mauritz I read about in the paper, the fighter pilot?" he wanted to know.

"That's me." I was beginning to get used to this sort of thing.

"Well, I think we might have been in the same place at the same time."

"Is that a fact," I answered. "I'd like to hear about it."

"Like I said, I was with the Rangers. I was taken prisoner at Cisterna and then taken to a camp in Laterina."

"When were you captured?"

"January of '44. The 30th of January, 1944. I think I was there, in that same prison camp, when you escaped."

Now I was very interested. "Can we meet somewhere?"

"Sure, I'll meet with you. And, Mike, the article said you escaped with a Ranger Captain. I think I know who that was."

"Yeah, what was his name?"

"Chuck," Larry said quietly. "Captain Chuck Schuster."

"That's right."

"Tough guy from Boston, but dead now. Quite some time ago," Larry added.

"Yes, I had heard that," I told him.

It was always important to me to provide Mariano de Pasquale and the people at Piana delle Orme with as much documentation as I could. I wanted them to be certain that everything I told them was the truth as well as I could remember it. That's why Lynn Gamma's documentation was important to me. It had occurred to me that there was probably no way to prove the details of my escape. But now Larry Schenkel had come into my life.

I liked Larry from the beginning. He had retained his

Ranger's edge and directness, and his talk was peppered with a gritty kind of humor that tickled me. After the preliminaries, Larry launched into his personal account, speaking in his gravelly, no-nonsense voice and ultimately providing the answer to what was, for me, one of the most nagging questions relating to our escape. With his permission, I tape-recorded his story:

"At ten or eleven in the evening of January 29, 1944, the Rangers were proceeding up to the town of Cisterna. Our object was to snap a rail line that led south to Casino. We went slowly through enemy lines. The Germans were to the right, along the Mussolini Canal. The operation was going well when, toward daylight, we spotted a German soldier fixing coffee or washing himself, something like that. We could see that there were more of them sleeping in foxholes. And some distance from them were four tanks. We halted. The Captain—it might have been Schuster, I'm not certain, but I know Chuck was somewhere in the vicinity, part of the operation—this Ranger Captain sent someone up to kill the German."

"How did he kill him?" I asked.

"With a knife. It was pretty quick, but the German, you know, he saw it coming and began pleading for his life. Well, that alerted the guys in the foxholes and they jumped up and started running for their tanks. None of them made it. We killed them all and then our bazooka people knocked the tanks out of commission. But all of this commotion brought other Germans into the area and our battalion commander shot up flares to notify our guys that we were now engaged in combat."

Larry told me he was certain he did not see Captain Schuster once the fighting actually started, so he couldn't say what happened to him during the confrontation. Then he went on, "Things got pretty heavy and rough. Our battalion commander was hit in the leg early on and he told us, 'Everybody's on their own, pass the word back.' I was leading a small group when we ran into a sergeant-major. We talked it over with him and decided to try to make it to this small outbuilding not far away."

Larry described a bloody standoff at the outbuilding, which, by early afternoon of the 30th, left three of their group dead and five others badly wounded. The wounded pleaded with those who were still able to fight to surrender. At last, unable to stand the suffering of their comrades, Larry and the sergeant-major decided that Larry should go for help.

"That was probably my first mistake," Larry said, describing how he stepped from the building and walked toward the barn where they had seen gunfire coming from both sides.

"There was this grape arbor that protected me as I walked. A few zings passed me by before I got to a fence near the barn and hollered, 'Does anybody speak English?'

"Two men came out. Germans. One was a big fellow, very tall and husky, who said, 'I speak better English than you do.'

"I was quick to tell him that I was an American soldier, because I knew the Nazis didn't hate us as much as they hated the British. Then the next thing this fellow says to me is, 'You have an accent.'

"'Okay,' I said to him, 'I come from the eastern part of the USA. You're from somewhere in Germany, you probably have an accent in German like I have an accent in English. What I'm here for is, I got wounded men up there in that building and I've got to get them some medical attention. Are you going to give me that?'

"'I'll take care of those men,' he said, 'as long as you don't fire at us.'

"I told him, 'They won't fire as long as I'm standing here with you.'

"Then he asked me, 'What do you got on the side of your hip there?'

Larry told the German that he carried a knife on one hip and a pistol on the other.

"'And what do you use that knife for?' he demanded.

"'To cut bread, slice open cans, you know.'

"'Look around you,' he ordered. But I wouldn't, because I knew what he wanted me to see. He wanted me to see all the Germans lying dead with their throats cut.

"I want to say this to you now, Mike. Yes, the Rangers were trained to kill in that way. We were sent into kill-or-be-killed situations. But we never killed in cold blood.

"The big English-speaking soldier then ordered me to toss him my knife and then my pistol. When he had the pistol in hand he removed the clip, which was empty. He tossed the clip in one direction and the pistol in another, saying, 'That's no good. It never was any good. We got the best pistol.'" (He was referring to the German Lugar, the prize that every American soldier wanted to bring home.)

Larry continued, "Then the German motioned to one of his men, saying, 'See that soldier out there on the road.' I looked toward a young officer facing me. The big German said, 'He's waiting for you. I'll take care of your wounded in the building.' I had no choice but to do as he said and hope for the best.

"I walked over to the soldier, who quickly dispatched others to gather those in our group who were uninjured. They ordered us into a little ditch and began discussing something. I noticed there were some German soldiers with automatic weapons looking down at us from the road above. Not far from me in the ditch was this young fellow who'd been born in Germany and came to the States as a boy. Under my breath I said to him, 'What are they talking about?'

"'They're talking about killing us,' he answered.

"Just what I thought. But at that very moment a vehicle came tearing up the road and a German officer jumped out. He was screaming at the German soldiers.

"'What's he hollering about?' I asked my buddy.

"'He's telling them to get us out of the ditch and up on the road.'

"I've often thought that if that officer hadn't come along, I'd have been a dead body in a ditch. That officer brought us to Cisterna, to a large three-story house where—"

"Wait!" I interrupted. "You said a three-story house in Cisterna?"

"That's right, and the commandant there spoke perfect English."

"So he must have been the same guy who gave me a pack of cigarettes. And there was a three-story building that was filled with Rangers. The place next door, too."

"That's it, Mike. It was all Rangers there, from that operation, you know. Captain Schuster was there. And he, I mean, Schuster was the commanding officer."

"Yeah, that was the place. Cisterna," I said.

"And then they bombed the hell out of us," Schenkel went on, "and they bombed us good."

"I was there then," I told Larry. "I was brought in shortly before the bombing. That's when I met Chuck. You must have been right there, maybe even in that room with the fireplace. They made me his interpreter since I could speak German."

"Oh, you speak..., well, that makes sense. I don't remember a fireplace. So that's how you and Chuck got to know each other."

"That's right. Now the next day, right, they took us to that railroad station near Rome and—"

"And our guys bombed us again. Yeah. But they were going for the tracks, to knock out the rail lines."

And so it went, Larry Schenkel and I matching our experiences moment to moment. We collected those old war fragments and put them together and they were a perfect fit. His and mine. Some parts were almost seamless. We talked about the march through Rome, our arrival at Laterina. Then, after fifty-four years, I was given the best gift of all: I got to hear what happened after we escaped.

"Let me back up a little," Larry said. "You see, every day, once we got to Laterina, I would see Chuck walking outside the barracks. You know how proud he was of his physique, so I figured he's walking to keep in shape and all. One day I joined him on his walk. I had always admired Chuck Schuster. You know, he couldn't have been more than twenty-four years old at the time and he had risen through the ranks. He was tough and daring. I mean, when there was something dangerous and difficult that had to be done, you could bet they'd give the job to Schuster. A real daredevil. And he demanded the same of his men. I guess you could say that a lot of guys respected him but didn't particularly like him, you know what I mean? He kept himself apart from everyone and you damn well knew he was out for himself. You could count on him 110 percent, but he wanted the glory for himself. Ego, you know.

"I remember one time when we were in training, we were being taught by the British commandos. There was a bunch of guys standing around, and Chuck, who always had to show off his strength and skill, handed me a knife.

"'Come on, Schenkel,' he says, with this weird, cold look in his eyes, 'come at me with that knife.'

"Well, I don't know if he thought I was crazy or what, but there was no way in hell I was going to put myself in that position. At the very least, I knew I'd be humiliated and at worst, I could have been hurt pretty bad, or maybe even killed. I was no match for him, even with a knife. He knew it and I knew it. But he just had to be better and tougher than everyone. He had to be admired and feared. You know, he had these great needs.

"So I said to him, 'No, sir, I won't do it. I know what you can do and I want to live to fight Germans.' Well, that kind of broke the ice and he smiled and that was that. But you see, he made his point with the other guys. That's all that mattered to him."

I told Larry that I knew exactly what he meant. And I shared some of my impressions about Schuster having some- thing of a dark past.

"Well, you know," Larry said, "he was this tough kid

who grew up on the streets of Boston. I don't think his childhood was the greatest. I think it was pretty rough and he was on his own at a very young age, I mean, he was just a kid. He bummed around a lot. But I'll tell you, my experience was that I'd rather be in combat with a guy who had that kind of street-smart survival instinct in him than any other kind of soldier. I had to admire that about Chuck. He really tried to make something of himself—you know how he became a bodybuilder and such a great athlete. And that was during the Depression.

"Once the war came, Chuck was in his element. The Rangers were the best thing that ever happened to him—making it all the way to Captain in an elite group like that, being a big war hero, carrying out all those daring and successful raids and missions. All that excitement and attention, and then it was over. After the war, he just couldn't get his life together. There are a lot of guys like that, who just can't make it in the civilian world or even in the peacetime military. It's not the same. Chuck just couldn't make the transition.

"After the war he got a call from Hollywood. They were making a movie about Colonel Darby and his Rangers, and they asked him to be a consultant on the film. Now, Chuck was a really good-looking man, I'm talking movie-star looks. He'd always said he wanted to get into the movies, and he really looked the part of the Ranger. I suppose Chuck thought this was his chance to make it into the movies—that's what I heard anyway. But he never did. Sad man, going from a great war hero to, well, not much. Of course he had a lot of friends and admirers. He did. I hope that before he died, he was able to put together some kind of life for himself…even if he just went back to cake decorating. You do know that's how he earned his living before the war?"

"Oh yeah. We talked about that some, especially when we were hungry," I said.

"Anyway, when Chuck and I were out walking that day in Laterina, we talked about our situation in the prison camp.

And he said to me, 'Do everything you can, Larry, to make life miserable for them.' He meant, you know, do the kinds of things that drive 'em nuts, just so long as you don't get killed. Give 'em the wrong information: if they tell you to walk left, go right, act really stupid, be a real pain.

"The next day I looked for him again, but Chuck wasn't out walking. I thought maybe something was funny. Then toward late afternoon or early evening we were all ordered outside to stand at attention. At first they weren't telling us anything. Then they told us that two men were missing and they wanted us to tell them who they were. You remember how disorganized they were. So that's when it dawned on me. Chuck, Captain Schuster, was one of the guys who got out. Good for him, I thought. That's why he gave me that advice about driving the guards crazy. As for those walks he was taking every day, I think he was casing the place, watching the guards, studying the fences, all that. But even if there were guys who knew for sure, of course no one was talking. So they had us stand there for a good long while, giving us hell and warning us not to try and escape, saying that they'd shoot two of us for every one that got out. You know the routine."

I felt so honored to have been given this incredible opportunity to look into the past. *Skipper* comes up from the deep and all of these people get interested enough to find me, and Larry Schenkel, of all people, contacts me! He had no idea what a gift he was giving me by telling me what happened after we left. No one was shot because of our escape. There was no great punishment because of our actions. This man had no idea how much I had wanted to hear this, but here he was, handing this to me.

After that, Larry told a grim story about the men being moved around, sometimes locked in freezing boxcars, once in open trucks, as they were taken through the Italian Alps. Many suffered frostbite and likely lost limbs. One time they boosted Larry up so that he could jump from the boxcar in order to unlock the door and free the men. He explained they were in a rail yard that was being heavily bombed. The men were trapped inside a death box. He did manage to get the boxcar open and the men scrambled out. They hid for a time in a basement and reemerged into a devastated German town, only to be recaptured and sent on their way again. The once-fit and rugged Rangers ended up sick, exhausted, and near death from starvation in a camp on the Russian front, in what was then Pomerania.

Life in that camp at least settled into a routine, with the occasional guard willing to grant favors in return for stuff that the prisoners could barter from their Red Cross packages, that is, if they were lucky enough to get their Red Cross packages. The Germans would often withhold the packages as punishment. But the enterprising Yanks still managed to set up a little black-market system to help get them through the misery of life as prisoners of war.

Hunger was always the greatest challenge in camp, according to Larry. "They might give us some potatoes to eat," he explained, "just plain potatoes still in their unwashed skins. Or bread sometimes, though it tasted like it was made with sawdust. Then there were the soups. They were made from potatoes or rutabagas, but I would only eat what I could skim off the top. If you dug down too deep, you'd come up with a lot of sand and dirt mixed in with the soup."

Larry always remembered Schuster's advice and did his best to harass the enemy. Some of the guards spoke English, and during long, cold nights in the camp, they would often engage the prisoners in conversation. The war-weary German soldiers, some of whom had been in the service for nearly a decade, all wanted to know the Americans' opinion of when the war would end. Larry would delight in sending a guard into deep depression by adopting a very serious and thoughtful air and assuring him that he had it on good authority that the war was likely to continue for another ten years.

Larry and the other Rangers remained prisoners until the late winter of 1945, when the Germans abandoned them one frigid evening, following a grim, three-and-a-half-month, four-hundred-mile walk back toward the Western front. The Russians arrived about six hours later, but the Rangers were not liberated for several weeks. During that time, rumors circulated that the Russians weren't going to release the Rangers.

Finally in May of 1945, almost a year after I returned home, Larry Schenkel and the others were repatriated. They had been prisoners for sixteen months.

The Invitation

In April of 1998 I received a letter from Italy on behalf of Signore Mariano de Pasquale, the owner of Piana delle Orme, the war museum that housed *Skipper*. The letter was written by Signore de Pasquale's assistant, Alda Dalzini, and translated by a retired Italian military officer and military historian by the name of Colonel Vasta. It seemed that Piana delle Orme Museum, which was located near the site of the Anzio invasion, was planning a three-day celebration in September to unveil *Skipper* in its new place of honor. Through Colonel Vasta, Alda went on to invite me and my family to be their guests at the celebration. She said it was their dream to "reunite man and machine."

I knew immediately that I wanted to go. And with just as much certainty, Louise knew that she did not. Oh, she was happy for me, but she felt that her health would prevent her from enjoying the trip. My son, Craig, his wife, Peggy, and my daughter, Donna, accepted right away. And so preparations began.

I would have loved experiencing this adventure with Louise, but Craig would make detailed videotapes of the entire trip, from the moment of our departure and in that way we would share it. In fact, those wonderful visual images and sounds that Craig faithfully captured would provide me with the inspiration and documentation necessary for me to write my thoughts, memories and feelings about my return to Italy.

The first face you see on the videos is that of my Louise. You can tell that she isn't used to saying goodbye to me. This moment isn't a happy one for her. She looks worried. She's fighting tears. But Craig, pointing the camera around the front yard from Louise to me to his sister, Donna, and wife, Peggy, is his usual relaxed and jovial self. "Look at those two," Craig says, focusing on the smiling Donna and Peggy, "off on the trip of a lifetime!"

Trying out the zoom on his new camera, Craig comes in close on me. I wave to the camera without smiling. It's hard for me to leave Louise; even for just a few weeks. We're not young any more. But I wanted very much to take this trip. Then, on the tape, Craig comments for posterity, "There he goes, Mum, a man on a mission!" Craig was right.

———

From the journals of Michael Mauritz, June, 1999; notes on his September, 1998, visit to Italy.

So many years had passed and the world had changed so much that our flight back to Italy seemed in no way connected to the war and *Skipper*. My children were in high spirits and our flight was a long, extended party interspersed with naps. We had been told that someone from the museum would meet us at the airport in Rome, but I was surprised and honored when we were greeted by three smiling men holding a large festive sign that read "Welcome, Lieutenant Mauritz!"

As we approached them, one of the men stepped forward and extended his hand to me.

"Welcome to Italy! How was your trip? Are you tired? Would it be all right if we went straight to the hotel? Signore de Pasquale is very anxious to meet you."

Craig's first shots of Italy are lovely. The countryside, taped from a moving car, has an abundant, lush greenness mixed with muted late-summer hues. The backdrop of mountains is a wash of misty purple, in striking contrast to the intense green of the fields. All of the plants and trees are tropical or evergreen. Houses, buildings, and businesses paint a picture of manicured prosperity. The Anzio area has done well from the time I first set foot here, scrambling out of the sea into the hands of my young German captor.

Next on the videotape you hear voices of a small crowd milling about in a room that has a slight echo. There I am, in the center of the crowd. It's easy to spot me, since I'm taller than most of the people who surround me. The camera shifts its focus to something crusted and rough. It's impossible to make out what it is, until Craig zooms out. It is the plane, my P-40L. It is *Skipper*. Sitting in a large sunken pool of fresh water, it has an other-worldly gold-green color. It has been fifty-four years since I watched it sink into the Bay of Anzio, and now here it sits, the crown jewel of the Piana delle Orme Museum. *Skipper* is surrounded by reporters, photographers, museum curators, Italian and U.S. Air Force brass, and historians. Presiding over the festivities is, of course, Mariano de Pasquale, Italy's fore-most flower exporter and creator of Piana delle Orme. It was Signore de Pasquale who financed the rescue of *Skipper* in order to present it to the world as part of his extensive collec-tion of World War II memorabilia, to be housed in the museum that is, for him, a dream come true.

But on this day everyone is here not just to see *Skipper* but also to meet its pilot. There are shots of me smiling, shak-ing hands, and talking to people through an interpreter who will be at my side during the whole trip. I was overwhelmed by the attention from the moment we arrived in Italy. I knew that the Italians were very interested in *Skipper*. I understood, too, their interest in me as the pilot who put it down in the bay. But I was not prepared for the reception I received. Neither was Craig, apparently, for he can be heard exclaiming on the video which he made for Louise, "Mum, Dad's as big as Madonna here! You can't believe all these people have come to see our Dad!" The people he refers to are photographers, videographers, newspa-per reporters, Italian military officials, people from NATO, and officials from the city of Anzio. But the person who stands out most is Mariano de Pasquale.

His people had taken care of everything. As soon as we arrived, we were taken to a beautiful hotel not far from Piana delle Orme. Waiting for us was Signore de Pasquale, the man who made all of this possible. He greeted us quietly and with great respect. He spoke through an interpreter, an Italian college professor named Dr. Gianni Blasi who speaks English like an American.

Craig's videotape of the first reception at Piana delle Orme features Angelo Silvestri, president of Archeosub, the organization of divers that brought *Skipper* up from the bay. Silvestri calls this meeting of man and machine a "dream come true." Dr. Blasi makes introductions and interprets, as dignitaries present me with plaques, photographs, decrees, and other honors. Then it is my opportunity to speak, with Dr. Blasi interpreting. "This is all beyond my imagination," I say. "I'm afraid I'm dreaming." I tell them that I feel blessed to have the opportunity to return in peace to this place where so many lost their lives.

From time to time Craig focuses his camera on Signore de Pasquale whose pride in this event is evident. But he is clearly a humble man, not one to seek center stage. Later on I will have the opportunity to get better acquainted with this self-made multimillionaire and world-renowned collector.

The camera now shifts outdoors to the museum's beautiful grounds for a celebration, which the people at Piana delle Orme have named "As If It Were Yesterday." A gray-haired gentleman in a finely tailored sports jacket is standing on a bandstand, speaking in a deep, soft voice—an Italian Barry White, Craig calls him. He takes his seat at the keyboard as the rest of the ensemble take their places. He gives a little downbeat and soon the crowd is enjoying a smooth, cool jazz number by these obviously accomplished musicians. After a few moments the music fades as Craig's voice offers up a stunning detail: the man with the gray hair, the keyboard player and band leader, is the youngest and only living son of the *Fascista* dictator Benito Mussolini!

After the concert there are more speeches and presentations of gifts. Next comes a grand dinner for several hundred. It is elegant, lavish, and, in perfect Italian style, it is fashionably late in getting underway.

"Look, Mum," Craig reports for his mother, "Dad's up five hours past his usual bedtime and he's drinking and having a ball."

It seems that everyone wants to talk with me. Cameras follow my every move. My interpreter Gianni, now joined by another, named Diego Cancelli, are at my side as I sign autographs and describe my feelings about reuniting with *Skipper*. I am asked again and again how I managed to put the plane down so skillfully in the bay, what was it like being captured, how did I escape.

When I read this it all sounds so egotistical, but no one was more surprised than I to find that there was such interest in my story. I know the interest wasn't just in me personally, it was in me historically and in my connection to the plane, to *Skipper*. And, of course, *Skipper* is a valuable addition to Piana delle Orme, and Piana delle Orme is important to the whole Anzio region as a link with history as well as a great tourist attraction.

Craig's videos show us enjoying many exquisite lunches and late-night dinners. In one, Craig focuses in on his sister sitting with three desserts in front of her and as many glasses of wine. Donna and Peggy, Craig's wife, have been enjoying every moment of their adventure and now the combination of wine and exhaustion is making them giddy. Craig notes that I have abandoned handshakes in favor of "Italian kissing," the kiss on each cheek, which is acceptable and even expected in Italy between friends and relatives, women to women, men to women, men to men. You know what they say: When in Rome...

At breakfast one morning, I sat with Signore de Pasquale on one side and Gianni Blasi on the other. Signora de Pasquale was seated on the other side of her husband. This was one of the smallest gatherings of the trip, so it gave Signore de Pasquale and me a chance to get to know each other. I also enjoyed getting to know Signora de Pasquale. I was touched when Signore de Pasquale asked his wife to show me her hands. They were the hands of a working woman, not the wife of a multimillionaire. "You see," Signore de Pasquale told me, "my wife has worked very hard to make a success of this business. She is the reason my business is so successful." You could tell that he is very proud of her and loves her very much.

Signore de Pasquale now got down to business. He produced a large paper shopping bag which aroused a lot of curiosity, even more so when he removed what appeared to be a large, dirty, ragged sheet. "Signore Mauritz," he began, "they pulled this parachute out of one of *Skipper*'s air-intake scoops. What do you make of it?" (Gianni was interpreting, but I already understood what Signore de Pasquale was asking.)

I answered through Gianni. "Tell them, Johnny, that this is not my chute. I swam ashore with my chute. I even swam back to the plane to get it, because it had gotten entangled in the cockpit. But I got the chute and waded ashore with it. I hid it under a bush and scrambled under another bush nearby. I had shed my Mae West and left it behind, but the German soldier who captured me didn't notice or care about that. He knew that my survival kit was in that chute which he found under the bushes and he knew that there would be some money in the kit. He asked me for the money. I even tried to buy my freedom with that money, but he said no."

Gianni, or Johnny as I was now calling him, listened as Signore de Pasquale responded, then turned back to me. "Signore de Pasquale says they think a saboteur put this chute in your scoop."

That was it! My plane had been sabotaged! That's why it overheated. "I've never understood why, until now," I told him. "I've heard people say that I was shot down. But I wasn't hit. I always knew that. I would have known if I had been hit. If there are any bullet holes in *Skipper*, they were there when I took off from Capodichino. Besides, *Skipper* could have taken a lot of hits without going down. Remember, those P-40's were heavy and tough."

After Gianni interpreted this for me, Mariano de Pasquale nodded in agreement and spoke briefly again. Gianni leaned forward and translated. Signore de Pasquale was saying that he knew that finding the parachute meant that *Skipper* had been sabotaged, but now my comments had confirmed it.

It was strange knowing for certain that my plane had been sabotaged. I knew that I hadn't been targeted personally. If the sabotage had been personal, it would have been directed against *Skipper*'s regular flyer, Lieutenant Parsons. I never knew Parsons or anything about him but sometimes guys got into terrible disagreements over gambling or women, or someone got it into his head that a fellow had carelessly endangered his life or the lives of his friends. These things happened. But I feel it is far more likely that the sabotage was the work of the enemy or enemy sympathizers. They just wanted to take out a plane and a pilot—any pilot. This was war, after all. And the greatest truth about it is that supposedly civilized people can become brutal and supposedly brutal people can perform acts of great civility. That's what happens in a war, and that's certainly what happened to me.

I had always believed and now, after fifty-four years, I was even more convinced, that my mechanic had done right by me in preparing *Skipper* for its last mission. I felt certain that sometime between the last check and takeoff, someone managed to slip onto the field and stuff a chute into the air intake.

––––––

On Sunday afternoon Piana delle Orme hosted an air show in my honor. Craig's camera captures me in the heat of a bright afternoon, surrounded by autograph seekers, shaking the hands of children, kissing babies.

While the NATO band performed for the air-show

crowd, I continued to be pursued by an enthusiastic group of newspaper photographers and television and radio reporters. Later my family and I paid our respects at a cemetery where a staggering number of American soldiers killed at Anzio are buried. The cemetery is a place of beauty with poplar trees standing guard over fountains, flowers, and grave after grave. I had the great honor of placing a wreath of flowers at the war memorial that was built by the United States.

Then our "entourage," as Craig jokingly called it, drove through the city of Nettuno en route to the Anzio war museum. There I was presented with a plaque from the city of Anzio along with framed photographs of the battle. As I listened to the presentation through Diego, who had taken over for Gianni on this occasion, I was anxious to speak.

Just before the presentation began, I had been introduced to an elderly man named Umberto Cappola. Diego told me that Signore Cappola had been in the army of Mussolini when Italy capitulated. Never a Fascist in his heart, the young Umberto volunteered to fight with the Allies. He assisted in supplying our troops at Anzio. He fought the long and bloody battles alongside the Allies until Italy was at last liberated.

The story moved me. Through Diego I asked many questions, and after a while Cappola and I were laughing and talking like old friends. I asked the photographers to take a picture of me with Signore Cappola. As we linked arms, I realized that it was the first time on this trip I had asked to be photographed.

When I was given the microphone, I wanted to set the record straight. I had been a fighter pilot, removed from the gritty reality of war. I wanted them to understand that at these many celebrations and ceremonies, I was only standing in for the thousands who suffered and died for the cause of freedom. "It was the ground troops who did the difficult work here...like this gentleman," I said, pointing to Signore Cappola. "I don't want to take the glory, because they deserve it."

When the ceremonies were over, I asked Diego to invite Signore Cappola to join me for the rest of the trip. Signore Cappola best represented the spirit of what I wished to convey on this trip, that of true solidarity and brotherhood. Governments have always waged wars over their differences. But the individuals, the human beings who fight and die in these wars, are not so different from one another. No, hardly different at all. Umberto Cappola could have walked away from the war after Italy capitulated. He could have just gone home and waited it out. But he chose to help us, the Allies, to bring the misery to an end. That's what I mean about the solidarity and brotherhood of all humans.

Craig's video next gives us a magnificent first sight of a postcard-perfect Italian hill town. This is the kind of place that painters paint and poets write about. We see sculpted fields of greens, gold, and russet. Ancient five- and six-story stone buildings with tile roofs rise up on the hillsides. Shuttered windows are dressed with flower boxes sending cascading flowers down the centuries-old walls. The September sun is intense as we wind our way up to the center of the town through the narrow streets alternately shaded and drenched in sunlight. This is Laterina, the prison town. How can it be that Nazi soldiers, and the *Fascisti* before them, brought their cold, hungry, and desolate prisoners to such a place of beauty and peace? But then, the fluttering umbrellas of Anzio's beach don't hint at the blood that soaked into that sand. That's the way it is with some of these places.

From the heart of Laterina which, as in many Italian hill towns, is at the highest point, we see a panoramic scene of fields, distant hills, and finally the ghostly hues of the Apennines rising in the background.

Looking at those distant peaks, I asked myself: How could Chuck Schuster and I have thought we could walk across those mountains all the way to the Adriatic Sea? Never mind the threat of being caught by the Germans or the *Fascisti*. The idea of crossing that range in winter with no compass, no gloves, nothing, astounds me.

In Laterina there was a news conference. The Italian media loved this story and *Skipper* and I seemed to be showing up in every newspaper, television and radio news program throughout Italy. The mayor of Laterina gave me a plaque, and through Diego, I thanked everyone and took questions from the press.

They wanted to know how the Ranger Captain and I escaped. Fortunately I had a diagram and was able to show them how we slipped unnoticed from barrack to barrack until we reached the last one. I told them about the two Italians working between the fences. I described the heart-stopping siren that turned out to be the signal for a lunch break. Then I talked about the muddy field and the Italian man we met just beyond the prison who assured us that he was no friend of the Germans. This was the man who rolled me a cigarette. Everyone laughed when I told them how the cigarette had made me dizzy and sick. But what I wanted most was for these and all Italians to know of the kindness and bravery their people showed us at the risk of their lives.

The journalists appeared to be enjoying themselves. Tape was rolling, notes were being taken, photos snapped. Finally, when the official presentation was finished, a man approached me and said, in Italian: "That was my father who rolled the cigarette for you."

I shook his hand, then hugged and kissed him.

Others came forward with photographs of their fathers, uncles, and grandfathers who fought in the war. It was important to them to make this connection with me. I had fought for the other side, but I believe that what we all shared in having experienced that war together is now larger than our differences ever were. We were young men caught up in the giant storm of a war that was not of our making. We did what we believed was the honorable thing in fighting for our countries. Now, as I see it, we are blood brothers in peace.

The town of Laterina hosted a grand luncheon for me, my family, and my new friends. Umberto Cappola sat near me. He had agreed to accompany me on the rest of our trip. I enjoyed his company. Language was no barrier for us two old soldiers.

At the end of the meal, I asked if I could go into the kitchen to thank the cooks. I like to do that. It's important to thank people who prepare food for you.

Roma

Rome is Rome. Whether it's captured in a postcard, a movie, a snapshot, or a video. Rome is glorious Rome. Writers may try to avoid using the word eternal to describe the city, because it is a cliché, but why fight it? Eternal *is* Rome. The wondrous ruins of an ancient greatness are as familiar to us as our own backyards. The steps, the fountains, the exquisite bodies in marble with their straight noses and perfect behinds, alongside their flesh-and-blood descendants sipping espresso, ogling the beautiful women who walk by, unfazed. Rome is elegant, bawdy, shabby, joyous, stylish, hectic, noisy, and exuberant. It was in the nature of this robust city to shed the aura of war quickly.

Looking at Craig's video, you see me standing, squinting into the sun with the Coliseum in the background. Craig explains, "Dad was here when he was a prisoner. This is where the march began."

As with all of the other historic sites on this journey, there seemed to be little connection between this place of such bleak memories and the place I was looking at now as a white-haired old man. War, all wars, occupied my mind that day and every day that I was in Italy. Throughout that glorious trip with all of the celebrations, the media attention, the sumptuous meals, and the treasured new friendships, I tried to remain focused on my reason for being in Italy and on the many, many thousands I represented who were not. It was certainly foremost in my mind during the visit to the American miliary cemetery at Anzio.

As my daughter, Donna, wrote after we returned home, "The most compelling experience of the trip was our visit to the cemetery with all the thousands of American soldiers buried there who never made it home. Each grave has a beautiful marble cross. It seemed as if we walked miles, looking at those crosses engraved with American names and hometowns.

It gives you a whole new outlook on the preciousness of life and the brutality of war. You hear war stories, read about them, and see films but to actually walk on the ground where these men (I should say *boys*) are buried, who gave their lives, who never made it home, is a feeling no words can explain."

At every stop in Italy, at every speech, I was given beautiful engraved plaques, lovely personalized mementos of the town or region, official declarations, all in commemoration of my war experience in Italy. But before I left Italy, I gave all of them to Signore de Pasquale to be displayed alongside *Skipper* at Piana delle Orme. I never lost sight of the fact that all of this fuss had nothing to do with me personally.

I often ask myself, So why did this happen to me? I mean, I was no hero. I didn't save anyone or suffer like so many others. Why did my plane surface and bring my story to light? I can only think that it is because I have a message of peace. I wanted Signore Cappolo with me because he was a man who had started out fighting on the opposite side in Mussolini's army. Then he was taken prisoner by the Allies and ended up fighting on our side. And he was down in the trenches, truly risking his life. When I met him, I was touched by his experience, by what he did. I felt a sense of brotherhood with him. I didn't feel that brotherhood with any of the high-ranking U. S., NATO, or Italian military. I felt it with Umberto Cappolo.

I believe I was called to tell my story because it's a tale of generosity and kindnesses, and people need to hear this kind of story. All of this giving and risking of lives for total strangers was happening at a time when evil was truly walking the earth. Doesn't that tell you something about the human heart?

They told us that the Germans were cruel and sadistic. That's what our government taught us. But so many of the individuals, these men and boys who were fighting in Hitler's army, had been given no choice. Of course, there were those who had it all wrong or made themselves blind to the blackness that had overtaken their government, but even some of these people could, and did, waken their hearts. The young German soldier who captured me could just as easily have shot me. But he didn't. The German soldier who gave me a blanket, or the one who gave me a loaf of bread—that was just basic human kindness. And how about the German officer who saved Larry Schenkel and the other Rangers from being massacred in a ditch near Cisterna? He did that only because he felt compelled to do what was right. What other motive could he have had for saving them?

I'll never know who among the wonderful Italians who helped us were truly on our side. Politically they could have been anything or nothing at all. But it doesn't matter. All that matters is that their goodness was called forth. When they saw someone who was hungry, they fed him. They gave him a safe place to sleep, dry clothes, and the warmth and safety of their kitchens.

God prepared me, I think, for this. He made me the typical American: born a Russian, baptized Russian Orthodox, raised a Roman Catholic by German-speaking Croatian parents, married to a Protestant, and finally a born-again Christian. You can't get much more American than that unless you can mix in some Jewish, African, Hispanic, Indian, and Asian blood. The twists and turns of my life have helped me to be able or willing to see things from many different angles.

I was no great hero. I did what I was told to do, and when things went wrong, I did what I had to do. But I always knew that I survived because of all the people who helped me. They were the heroes. And I had the great good fortune to be in their company.

Stato della Citta del Vaticano

When they told me that we were going to be meeting the Pope, I thought immediately of what you see on television. I figured they meant we would be part of the crowd watching the Pope come out on his balcony to bless the thousands in the square below. But Diego explained that it would be an actual face-to-face meeting, very brief but very real nonetheless. He said the Pope would pray with me, so I should decide what I wanted him to pray about.

I thought, of course, of Louise and our family. But then I started thinking about what had brought me here. A war, initially. But the kindness that was extended to me from people I was told were my enemies taught me that the capacity for peace is within everyone. It's war that's unnatural and inhuman. So I figured that I must ask this good man to pray with me about peace.

When the day came to meet the Pope, we were all quiet as we entered Vatican City. Our friend Diego was with us as interpreter and guide. September 9, 1998, was another bright, hot Roman day as we came through the ancient walls and into the Vatican City, the *Citta del Vaticano.*

This place, we learned, was once the site of the emperor Nero's public gardens. Countless early Christians had died here. But it is the belief that Saint Peter was crucified on what is now called Vatican Hill and is buried nearby that makes this a holy place.

The thought that the great Saint Peter walked on this ground thrilled me. How can you not love the big, rough, and impetuous fisherman who was always first to express his love for Jesus and just as often said or did the wrong thing? He was flawed by his denial of Jesus, but forgiven. Flawed but forgiven—just like us. Peter. The "rock." I was sure that his great presence made the very dust of this place touched by heavenly grace.

The Basilica of Saint Peter looms like a giant over all the beautiful buildings, gardens, and courtyards of the Vatican. The symbolism is perfect. Although it was a weekday and not a special holiday, Vatican City was filled with people who, once inside the great walls, are referred to as pilgrims. I like the notion of being a pilgrim, someone who is willing to struggle and sacrifice but plugs along, toughs it out, and makes the journey, knowing how worthwhile the end will be.

My pilgrimage to that holy place had taken me on a journey along a twisting, turning path, a journey that began a long time ago in Pennsylvania. It took me through a thunderstorm that changed and probably saved my life. It took me through a good and nurturing childhood with two loving parents. It took me to flight school and into the great blue bowl of heaven. It took me across the ocean, through a desert, to the fires of war. It took me down into foreign waters and up to snow-capped mountains. It took me to the doorsteps of people who gave me food and shelter at the risk of their own lives. It taught me the true meaning of "brotherhood of man." It brought me back home again and gave me the joy of seeing relief and gratitude on the faces of my mother and father. It took me through sweet romance, a treasured marriage, and the joys and challenges of fatherhood. It took me through middle age and the working world. It took me through a renewal of my spirituality and faith. Now as life's journey requires me to wear bifocals to read the morning paper and study the faces of my grandchildren, my step may have slowed a little but this pilgrim is still an intrepid traveler, always anxious to see what's around the bend. So when *Skipper* surfaced and I found myself on my way back to Italy, I felt that I was approaching something big and important in my journey. And I was.

On the day that we met the Pope, we brought special

documents that allowed us to go toward the front of the square nearest the place where the Pope would emerge. We lined up. I was number thirteen in line.

The face of Pope John Paul II is a combination of strength and frailty. As you approach him, the ravages of life and time are what you notice first. But the steady, bright light and the peace in his eyes and on his face is fresh and vibrant. A young and vigorous spirit lives in that beleaguered body.

The great man, who has had a personal experience with war and oppression, nodded and smiled when I asked if we could pray for world peace and brotherhood. The power of his prayer was a very real thing. Something great and strong came to attend us. It was over in seconds, but the sense that a presence was with us will remain with me forever.

The day I met the Pope was a great one in my life. I never dreamed I would have such an opportunity, such a gift. While I was experiencing the joy of his presence in one of the earth's holy places, a part of my story was unfolding in heaven, though I wouldn't know of it immediately.

Sometime after I returned home, I was reading a newsletter for Air Force veterans. In a section called Folded Wings, I read that Major Melvin Nielsen had died—my formation leader on my last assignment over Anzio. He was the one I spoke to on the radio to report that my engine was overheating. He was the only one who knew that I was going to try an emergency landing in the bay. It was Nielsen who circled back at his own peril, watched me scramble ashore at Anzio, and saw the young German officer approaching my hiding place in the bushes. He saw *Skipper* go under, radioed for the launch to rescue me, and took the time to write the report that told me, fifty-four years later, all that had been done to help me. It was Major Nielsen's report that filtered back to my birth family through my brother-in-law, letting them know that I survived the crash landing and had likely been taken prisoner.

It was also Major Nielsen's report that supported my

story and gave me confidence that Signore de Pasquale and the others at Piana delle Orme had everything they needed to give credence to the facts of my war experience, my story. Until they saw that report, everything they knew from the moment I went down until I returned behind lines five months later was my word. It was as true an account as I could possibly give, based on my memory and knowledge. But the efforts of the people at Piana delle Orme to present me to the Italian media deserved to be supported by indisputable fact.

The Air Force newsletter reported that Major Nielsen had passed away on September 9, 1998, the very day I had visited and prayed with the Pope.

Perhaps it's a coincidence with no important meaning. Still, I see something there. I believe that heaven sends us little signals sometimes and that this was one of them, this little constellation of events and people that seemed unconnected to one another and yet came together perfectly. The man who saw me wash up on a distant shore was himself reaching that other great distant shore on a day when our shared experience was very much in my heart. Although I've prayed for him often since reading his obituary, I like to think that my little prayer with the Pope on the day Major Nielsen died served him as well as his faithfulness had served me the day that *Skipper* went down.

In the Fullness of Time

Michael Mauritz and his family returned home from Italy, bringing with them the lasting love and friendship of the many good people he had met through the celebration of *Skipper* at Piana delle Orme. There would be more newspaper articles about *Skipper* and its pilot in the Pittsburgh papers, and they would always be followed by a flurry of calls and letters from veterans and military aircraft enthusiasts. Meanwhile, Boyd Fallwell's Web site reported on Michael's trip. All of this publicity as well as the many newspaper, magazine, and television stories about Michael and *Skipper* led to more articles in foreign magazines. Michael regularly receives e-mail messages, faxes, and letters from all over the world. He often reflects on the appeal of his story of a war plane that returned from the sea after fifty-four years.

"What is it people like about this story so much?" he asks. "Well, maybe it's just that everyone likes a love story."